The story of ANTIQUES

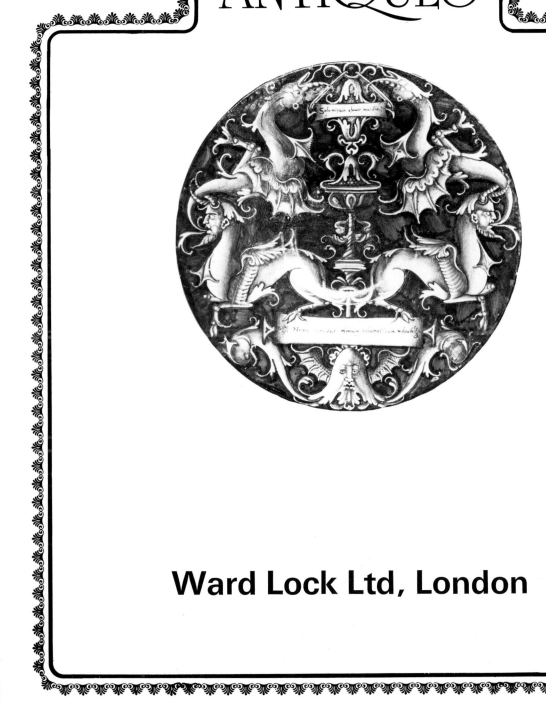

Ward Lock Ltd, London

The story of ANTIQUES

June Glencross

Acknowledgements

The publishers gratefully acknowledge the following who have supplied the illustrations for this book:
By gracious permission of HM the Queen 55, 115; The American Museum in Britain, Claverton Manor, Bath 39tr, 81t, b, 94b, 118t, 130; Gemeentemuseum Arnhem 108t; Bayerisches National-Museum, Munich 85bc; Barber Institute of Fine Arts, Birmingham 93b; Kupferstichkabinett der Oeffentlichen Kunstsammlung, Basel 15; Museum of Fine Arts, Boston 92b; The Trustees of the British Museum 36t; The Brooklyn Museum, New York 111b; Centraal Museum, Utrecht 44r; Chequers Trust 41l; City Museum and Art Gallery, Birmingham 14t, 141t; City of Cardiff Corporation 124; Cooper Colour Library 118b; Corporation of the City of London 109b; Country Life 31, 125; The Marquess of Exeter 31; Photographie Giraudon 61b; Glasgow School of Art 127t, 128, 134l; The Worshipful Company of Goldsmiths, London 9l, 27, 138; R. Guillemot 34; The Hamlyn Group Library 16b, 17tl, tr, b, 38t, 40l, 64l, 66l, 88tr, 103l, 106, 107, 119, 135t, b, 137t, b; Michael Holford 18t, b, 51, 58t, 75r, 86bl, 90, 94t, b, 95t, 118t; A. F. Kersting 57, 73, 74l, r, 120; Kunsthistorisches Museum, Vienna 23; Robert Lehman Collection, New York 9r; The Earl of Leicester, Holkham Hall, Norfolk 60; Claire Leimbach 126t, b; The Trustees of the London Museum 22b; Louvre, Paris 58b, 69tr, 103r; Musée National du Château de Malmaison 98, 108; Metropolitan Museum of Art, New York, Joseph Pulitzer Bequest 92t, 93tr; The National Gallery, London 59t; National Maritime Museum, Greenwich 36b; National Museum of Ireland 97bl, br, 112tl, tr, b; The National Trust 14br, 30b, 32, 35r, 39l, br, 51, 94t, 95t; The Marquess of Northampton 122t; The Earl of Pembroke, Wilton House 30t; Rijksmuseum, Amsterdam 35l, 40b, 43br, 46r, 47l, 65r; Royal Institute of British Architects 101t, b, 114b; The Royal Pavilion, Brighton 99, 114t, 115; Royal Scottish Museum, Edinburgh 45bl; Sächsische Landesbibliothek, Dresden 25l; Scala, Florence 19t, 26b, 82, 85t; Musée National de Céramique, Sèvres 67l; Staatliche Kunstsammlungen, Dresden–Grünes Gewölbe 69tl; The Tate Gallery, London 59b; Thames and Hudson Ltd. 7; Trans-Globe Film Distributors Ltd. 19b, 35t, 60; Transworld Feature Syndicate 19b; The Trustees of Sir John Soane's Museum 80cl; Victoria and Albert Museum, London 6l, 8, 10, 11, 13, 14t, 16t, 17c, 18br, 19l, r, 22t, 24l, 25t, br, 29l, t, 42tl, bl, r, 43t, bl, 44t, 45tl, r, 46l, 47r, 48tl, tr, b, 49l, r, 52t, b, 53tr, bl, br, 54, 62t, bl, 63, 66r, 67r, 69bl, br, 70, 71l, tr, 75l, 77t, b, 78t, b, 79t, b, 80tr, b, 82, 83, 84b, 85bl, 86t, bl, 87, 88l, 89t and detail, 90, 91, 93tl, 94b, 95t, 96, 97t 104l, r, 105, 111tl, tr, 113 116, 117l, tr, br, 119, 121, 122b, 123tl, tr, bl, br, 127b, 131, 133t, bl, br, 142, 143, 144t, bl, br; The Trustees of the Wallace Collection, London 6r, 20l, 24r, 26t, 28, 29cr, 33, 38l, 41r, 44l, 50, 61t, 62r, 64r, 65l, 68, 76t, b, 84t, 85br, 86br, 132; Josiah Wedgwood & Sons Ltd. 88br; Wellington Museum, London 110; L. Wittamer-de Camps, Brussels 139b; Kunstverlag Wolfrum, Vienna 37.

ISBN 0 7063 1207 4
Published by Ward Lock Limited
Designed and produced by
Trewin Copplestone Publishing Ltd, London
© Trewin Copplestone Publishing Ltd 1973
Printed in Spain by
Printer Industria Gráfica SA, Tuset 19, Barcelona
San Vicente dels Horts
Depósito legal B18971-1973
Mohn Gordon Ltd, London

Page 1 Italian maiolica: plate decorated with grotesques, made at Deruta, near Perugia, about 1515

Page 3 French mantel clock, with the movement in a globe of black enamel. The gilt figure of Minerva counsels the young King Louis XVI. Second half of the 18th century

Contents

Introduction   6

The sixteenth century   12

The seventeenth century   32

1700–1750   56

1750–1800   72

1800–1840   98

1840–1910   120

Cutlery 1500–1800   48
Musical instruments 1500–1800   52
English clocks 1700–1900   116
Some musical instruments after 1800   144

Introduction

Most people today value what is old; antiquity is respected for its own sake. 'Five hundred years old' says the guide, and his audience will look in the direction he is pointing with a kind of hushed awe. Often we are so pre-occupied thinking how old an object is, we forget to stop and consider how good it is.

Loving what is old, we have–more than any previous generation–a tremendous enthusiasm for antiques. Suppose, however, it were possible for us to walk into the study of some enlightened Italian Renaissance duke (and a very splendid study it might be, for such a man would like to have his taste, his interests, perhaps even his way of thinking, reflected in his surroundings–so it seems the Duke Federico da Montefeltro did in his intricately inlaid Studiolo at Urbino). Suppose we told him of our enthusiasm. He would at first regard us with some surprise (for it was a new idea to investigate and collect what was old) and he would then enquire how we had come by this burning passion for the works of ancient Greece and Rome? From then on we should be at cross purposes, for this was how the term 'antiques' would be understood in Renaissance Italy. The sculptor Pier Jacopo Alari Bonacolsi, working in Mantua in the late fifteenth and early sixteenth centuries, was also a collector of ancient Roman carvings. These he admired for other qualities than their antiquity. Indeed, he modelled his own work upon them, and gained himself the nickname 'Antico.'

Italian maiolica dish, 1480–1500, with sgraffito (incised) design of two youths in a garden

Left 'Meleager' in parcel-gilt bronze by Antico, late 15th or early 16th century

Opposite page Duke Federico da Montefeltro's study at the Palazzo Ducale, Urbino, Italy: a brilliant use of 'trompe-l'œil' inlay

Anywhere else but in Renaissance Italy, the name would have been considered far from flattering. 'Antique' was then much the same word as 'antick' or 'antic' – that is to say, something not only old-fashioned but grotesque, ridiculous and incongruous.

I suppose we know well enough today what we mean by 'antiques'. Or do we? To qualify as an antique an object must, in the broadest sense, be a work of art, of what we call applied art. It is something more than just a chance survival from a past generation, a 'bygone', to use the museum curator's term. It should also be, again in the broadest sense, portable – that is to say, while it may need four strong men to stagger across the room with it, it should not be part of an architectural structure – not a column, or a mosaic, or a stained glass window, or a large-scale piece of wrought-ironwork.

Among his other commendable enterprises, Duke Federico built on the rugged site of Urbino a palace which many believe to be the most beautiful in all Italy; and he furnished it so well and appropriately that it seemed more like a city than a mere palace. For he adorned it not only with the usual objects, such as silver vases, wall-hangings of the richest cloth of gold, silk and other similar material, but also with countless antique statues of marble and bronze, with rare pictures, and with every kind of musical instrument; nor would he tolerate anything that was not most rare and outstanding. Then, at great cost, he collected a large number of the finest and rarest books, in Greek, Latin and Hebrew, all of which he adorned with gold and silver, believing that they were the crowning glory of his great palace.
From Baldassare Castiglione's *The Courtier*, written between 1508 and 1518.

It used to be said, not very many years ago, that to be classified as an antique a thing had to have been made before 1830. And if one asked, why 1830 in particular?–the reason given was that that was the date when industrialism really set in. But this argument fails to take two things into account: first, that industrialism may produce works of art, even if this does not happen as often as one would wish: second, that because they live in an industrial age people do not immediately and entirely desist from throwing pots, weaving fabrics and exercising their craftsmanship in wood and silver and glass.

The next age limitation made for antiques was that they must be at least a hundred years old. This definition, when one comes to think about it, is even more absurd because it is even more arbitrary; it allows us to recognise the earlier works of William Morris as 'antiques', but for another two or three decades Art Nouveau will still be beyond the pale! One has to draw a line somewhere, and for the purposes of this book, it is drawn (rather waveringly) in the vicinity of 1910, because with the final flourishings of Art Nouveau and the closing of at least the first phase of the Arts and Crafts movement, there does seem to have been then something like the end of an era.

But there has to be a starting-line as well as a finishing-line; and this has been drawn (rather reluctantly) about 1500. Earlier than this, the applied arts were certainly flourishing and were highly esteemed, too–no-one looking at the painting of St Eligius and St Godeberta by Petrus Cristus, with its loving and delicately-drawn array of them, could doubt that. And this standing cup and cover crowned with a virgin and unicorn, and made in England for the Mercers' Company, indicates a long and splendid tradition of metal-work. But what has survived from medieval times and earlier has a secure niche in our art galleries and museums, and is seldom there to tempt the collector in the antique market.

Not that this book is much concerned with the buying and selling of antiques, or with their current commercial values. It is far more concerned with the enjoyment of the things for their own qualities, and one can have this pleasure whether one actually possesses the objects or not, whether the price is or is not beyond one's pocket. But to derive the greatest enjoyment from them, one needs to see them against the setting of the times in which they

Left Roundel in enamelled terracotta, about 1460, by Luca della Robbia: it depicts the month of May

Opposite page left English standing cup and cover, silver gilt with translucent enamel, 1499

Opposite page right Detail of goldsmith's work from 'St Eligius and St Godeberta' by Petrus Cristus, 1449

were made; one needs to know something of the artistic trends which prevailed then, of the taste which made men choose one line or one shape rather than another.

Then one can look at them, not just as a form of commercial currency exchanged by a certain élite, but with new eyes; one can appreciate their real worth just as if they were paintings or sculptures or any other work of art.

There is nothing magical about the year 1500 (apart from the fact that many people immediately before that date expected the world would end then); in the history of art, it marked the high point rather than the beginning of an era. This was nowhere more true than in Italy, where already work in the visual arts was far more highly evolved than in any other country. A measure of excellence had been found. Man thought rather less of divine judgement and rather more of his own. His position in the scheme of things was, he now believed, central. That is not to say that the humanists of the early Renaissance denied the existence of God, but rather that they emphasized the importance of man, man as an individual, thinking and not altogether uninfluential being. And his passage through this world was no longer held to be just a brief prologue to eternity. Brief it might be, but how much might be achieved during it? And how civilized might it be made?

With these thoughts in mind, it is not surprising that in fifteenth-century Italy men — if they had means enough — should set about making their surroundings, and everything they used and possessed, as beautiful as possible. Still not much troubled with the profounder doubts and probings and questionings which were to come later, they did this with gaiety and freshness. A brave new world had rediscovered an old one, and the wonder of this was implicit in almost every work to which man turned his hand.

So Luca della Robbia persuaded clay to do more vivid and delightful things than it had ever done before. And he not only inspired the potters of Faenza in particular with a new vision, but instructed them in a new technique — that of an opaque tin-enamel glaze which, combined with other chemicals, would fire to a brilliant range of colour.

Furniture, too, began to assume a new splendour. Concerned rather with transforming the apparent nature of wood than with bringing out its grainy characteristics, craftsmen painted and gilded their more ambitious pieces – until one is unaware, for instance, that a certain Florentine marriage-chest is in fact made of walnut, because one is so taken up with a fascinating portrayal of fifteenth-century courtly life which masquerades as Solomon's meeting with the Queen of Sheba.

Florentine cassone (marriage-chest), walnut, painted with a scene of Solomon meeting the Queen of Sheba. From the workshop of Apollonio di Giovanni (1415–65)

Enough has survived from the early Italian Renaissance for us to be able to make some generalizations about it. In fact, we are in a better position to do so than any one man living at the time. It must not be forgotten that the difficulties of travel and the existence of city-states as more or less self-contained units, discouraged or even denied the possibility of wide artistic experience. It was the quality, not the quantity of that experience which was the thing.

This is Guarino of Verona (who was a humanist, a scholar, and as intellectually and visually aware a person as one could hope to meet in the mid-fifteenth century) writing to the sender of a present:

Not to speak of almost countless other things, how could I find words and style worthy of the ink-stand you sent me? Though certainly its form is most beautiful, elegant, and apt, this is overshadowed by the truly Phidian skill and workmanship I feast my eyes on. If I fix my gaze on the leaves and little branches and look at them attentively, shall I think I am looking at real leaves and real branches and that they could be safely bent this way and that? So does the diligence of Art seem to rival the ease of Nature. Often I cannot have enough of the pleasure I find in examining the little figures and the living faces in the clay ... Nails, fingers and hair, soft even though earthen, take me in when I behold them. When I look at an open mouth I expect a voice to come from the dumb; when I see the putti hanging from the tree I forget that they are made of earth and fear they may fall and injure their small bodies, and I call out in pity.

This must rate as one of the most enthusiastic thank-you letters ever written. When we read it today there are at least three points which strike us as interesting, even surprising. First, that this effusion is unleashed not by a painting or a sculpture but by a piece of applied art, a maiolica inkstand differing probably only in detail from the one on page oo. Second, that the inkstand was not what we should call an antique but a piece of 'modern' craftsmanship – if it had been old, he would probably not have thought so much of it. Thirdly, not once in this long passage does he mention the name of the artist-potter who made it. The work clearly captured Guarino's imagination; to us it seems odd that its creator should be of such small account.

Italian sgraffito maiolica inkstand. Bologna, about 1500

The sixteenth century

The anonymity of the fifteenth-century potter could never have done for Benvenuto Cellini (1500–1571), Florentine sculptor and goldsmith – probably the finest goldsmith the world has ever produced. His autobiography, a delightful racy and ebullient work, leaves us in no doubt as to the high opinion the man had of himself. Tolerating the patronage of Popes and princes, so he would have us believe, only as long as it suited him, he held his status to be only slightly inferior to that of the great Michelangelo.

The career of Cellini, while a disreputable one in some ways, made it possible for the goldsmith to aspire to a higher level of society than he had before. His art, along with the other applied arts, had always been well thought of. Indeed, up to about 1500 little distinction was made between the 'fine' and 'applied' arts. Many eminent sculptors and painters had received some training in 'applied' arts and this could be a formative influence. This was true north of the Alps as well as south of them: Albrecht Durer, who was trained as a goldsmith, is a case in point. But by the time of the High Renaissance, around 1500, it was recognized that the artist, as well as what he produced, had individuality and importance. At first this only applied to the painter, the sculptor, the architect. Cellini, though he did not quite succeed in equating him with these, certainly brought the worker in applied arts out from behind his bush.

It was the new idea of man's place in the scheme of things which was more crucial to the Renaissance than the revival of Roman art-forms. Classical decorative designs, consisting of the stringing together of such motifs as medallions, goats' masks, sphinxes and foliage, the whole effect rather understated but very delicately balanced, had been discovered in such places as the Golden House of Nero in Rome. Because the level of the streets of Rome had risen with the deposits of centuries, these ancient apartments had, by the sixteenth century, become subterranean grottoes; so the designs found in them were called 'grotteschi', or grotesques. Raphael was among the first of the Renaissance artists to adapt them for his own decorative schemes. Cellini favoured them too, though he thought the term a misnomer and preferred to call them 'arabesques'. Such designs, he declared, based on the acanthus plant and interspersed with birds and animals (as used by the best artists of Rome and Tuscany), were superior to those used by the artists of Lombardy which were based on the forms of bryony and ivy, beautiful though they were. And both, he felt, were infinitely more satisfying than Islamic decoration, which he had observed on some damascened Turkish daggers. 'Turkish arabesques', he wrote, 'are only composed of arum leaves with a few sunflowers; and though they have a certain grace, they do not yield so lasting a pleasure as the patterns which we use.'

The rest of Europe was, as a whole, inclined to agree with Cellini on this point. The arts of all those countries which counted themselves in any degree civilized were touched by Italian Renaissance, and therefore ultimately by classical, design. Sometimes it might be combined rather oddly with Gothic, or in Spain with Islamic, forms, often it was ill-digested, crudely conceived; but it was there.

In England, for instance, the increasing wealth and influence of the middle classes, especially, was reflected in a general rise in living standards. 'The furniture of our houses also exceedeth', wrote William Harrison in his *Description of England*, 1587, 'and is grown in manner even to passing delicacy; and herein I do not speak of the nobility and gentry only, but likewise of the lowest sort in most places of our south country that have anything at all to take to. Certes in noblemen's houses it is not rare to see abundance of arras, rich hangings of tapestry, silver vessel, and so much other plate as may furnish sundry cupboards to the sum oftentimes of a thousand or two thousand pounds at the least.' But knights, gentlemen and merchants also strove to equip their houses splendidly, and often was 'their great provision of tapestry, Turkey work, pewter, brass, fine linen and thereto costly cupboards of plate, worth five or six hundred pounds.' Even farmers and craftsmen had begun 'to garnish their cupboards with plate, their joined beds with tapestry and silk hangings, and their tables with carpets and fine napery.' But in matters of design it was towards Renaissance Italy that men looked for inspiration; for there, it was felt, they had the pattern for civilized living.

At Fontainebleau in France, the influence was more direct and rather different. The king, François I, imported from Italy prominent artists such as Rosso, Primaticcio and Niccolò dell'Abbate to decorate his palace there in the newest fashion. The newest fashion was what we now call Mannerism – a style more vigorous than relaxed, more exaggerated than harmonious, varying between the elegance of elongation and the forcefulness of compression. Fontainebleau in its turn, until well into the seventeenth century, had a considerable influence on the arts in the rest of Europe.

The spread of these styles from one country to another was made both easier and quicker when the invention of printing was added to the art of engraving. For we must remember that this was long before the days of exhibitions; a work of art, once created, was likely to remain in its place of origin. Few artists travelled abroad, as Dürer did, to see for themselves the work being done in other countries. It is true that earthenware dishes (especially Italian maiolica ones, where the decoration was often based on paintings by the great Renaissance masters such as Raphael) could serve as a form of colourful and portable – though not always accurate – reproduction, and that earlier, in the Middle Ages, the transporting from country to country of tapestries and illuminated manuscripts had resulted in there being some common currency of style, but the importance of printing, which made easier the transmission of ideas, in addition to engraving which was now used increasingly for the transmission of images, can hardly be overestimated.

Knot design by Albrecht Dürer: the First Knot

The sixteenth century

The Long Gallery, Aston Hall, Birmingham, England

Detail from 'Birth of the Virgin', woodcut by Albrecht Dürer, 1502–5

Elizabethan windporch, Montacute, Somerset, England. 'Strapwork' is combined with French Renaissance detailing

Furniture

Walking into a room, even a room in a palace, set out and equipped just as it was in the sixteenth century, one would be struck by the sparseness, by the generally uncomfortable nature, of its furnishings. Very seldom did the master of the house have an upholstered chair to sit on, though he might well have one which was elaborately carved and turned; other members of the household might count themselves lucky if they had stools. Tables were often no more than trestles, chairs were also moveable, so any room could serve as a dining-room, and most rooms (except, for instance, the Italian lord's study) were general-purpose living-rooms. In Holbein's drawing, the family of Sir Thomas More is seen in a room of this sort.

Perhaps because the actual constructional craftsmanship was often rather crude, there was a tendency in the early years of the century to cover it up, whether by painting it or by draping it with Turkey carpets. The carpets were, of course, much too precious to be trodden on. Rather than invest much in comfort (though comfort is a comparative term, and to medieval eyes Renaissance apartments would have seemed luxurious in the extreme), sixteenth century man preferred – if he could afford them – to have just a few really magnificent pieces of furniture. In many countries, England among them, the most splendid piece in the house was often the bed; even the second-best bed, such as Shakespeare left his wife, might be quite a valuable affair.

In Italy, the piece on which the most loving craftsmanship was lavished was generally the *cassone* or marriage-chest. Italian brides were (and in some places probably still are) expected to bring with them a considerable trousseau, including linen enough to last all their married life. This would be placed in one, or more often

The Family of Sir Thomas More, drawing by Hans Holbein showing English 16th-century furnishings

The sixteenth century

two, of these decorative containers. The word *cassone* simply means a large box or chest, however, and later on these ornamental objects seem to have been put to practical use as receptacles for all manner of clothes and household effects. In the early Renaissance, *cassoni* were usually painted. Then the painting was superseded in northern Italy by inlaid work and in the south by opulent carving with sometimes the addition of gilding.

The English equivalent (though they had, as far as we know, no nuptial connotations) were the so-called Nonesuch chests, so-called because nineteenth-century antiquarians thought that the marquetry designs on them represented Henry VIII's fantastic palace in Surrey. In fact, these decorative panels show no more than architectural caprices; similar chests were made in Germany, particularly Augsburg.

The decoration of really splendid furniture, was not something that even the greatest of artists necessarily felt beneath their dignity to do. We know that Giovanni Bellini painted furniture panels, and we have from Holbein's hand a wonderfully intricate table-top which he executed for Hans Baer and his wife Barbara Brunner of Basle.

In France, furniture was principally indebted to the architect (while in other countries it might owe much in its design to the painter or to the sculptor). A dresser was something on which the designer might display his knowledge of the five orders of classical architecture; and if a table was required to be a more impressive affair than the old functional trestle, columns and piers and arcades might transform it into a miniature building.

North Italian cassone of walnut inlaid with other woods and ivory, about 1500

Below Designs for beds by Hans Vredeman de Vries, from his pattern-book of about 1580

French 16th-century table of architectural form, adapted from a design by Ducerceau

'Caquetoire' or gossiping chair in carved oak. Second half of the 16th century

Roman cassone (marriage-chest), walnut carved and partly gilt. Third quarter of the 16th century

Folding hip-joint chair, Spanish. First half of the 16th century

Most sixteenth-century furniture was indeed heavy in style. Almost the only exceptions were some of the smaller chairs. The French, from their heavier throne-like chairs, developed the *caquetoire* or 'gossiping' chair with its seat narrow at the back but wide enough in front to accommodate stiff or voluminous skirts. In Spain they made folding hip-joint chairs, which were practical as well as decorative, being easy to carry from room to room.

In matters of design, Spain—now entirely freed from Moorish rule—increasingly abandoned Islamic patterns and assumed an Italian type of design, which in fact most of Europe was trying, more or less successfully, to emulate. In the northern countries, however, there were as a counter-influence pattern books such as those

The sixteenth century

Above and left Galérie François I, Fontainebleau, France, constructed 1533–40, with fresco and stucco decoration by Rosso Fiorentino

Below 'Nonesuch' chest of oak inlaid with other woods. English, 16th century

Above Casket in silver-gilt, carved rock-crystal and enamel, made by Valerio Belli and presented by Pope Clement VII to François I of France in 1532

Below Painted Staircase, Knole, Sevenoaks, Kent, England. 1604

The sixteenth century

of Vredeman de Vries, and elements from both sources were often combined in one piece of furniture. Northern and southern Europe also differed as to choice of woods: in the north, oak was still the most popular wood; in the south, walnut was in favour. It was largely a question of availability, rather than an embodiment of regional characteristics.

Ceramics

The sixteenth century saw the development of tin-glazed earthenwares. The addition of tin oxide to a lead glaze on earthenware gave an opaque, enamel-like surface, which could be painted with oxides or enamel colours – producing an effect of unprecedented brilliance. In Italy, such wares were called *maiolica* (people thought they had come from Majorca; in fact, the technique had been introduced from the Middle East, largely through Spain), in France they were called *faïence* (from Faenza in Italy), in Holland and Great Britain *delft* (after Delft in Holland, of course). Essentially, these are three different names for the same thing.

The technique had its finest flowering in sixteenth-century Italy. The methods used there were set down by one Cipriano Piccolpasso of Castel Durante in his *Three Books of the Potter's Art*, and we learn that the range of colours used were cobalt blue, antimony yellow, iron red, copper green, manganese purple and also white

French Limoges enamel dish, late 16th century. The design is based on Raphael's 'Triumph of Galatea'

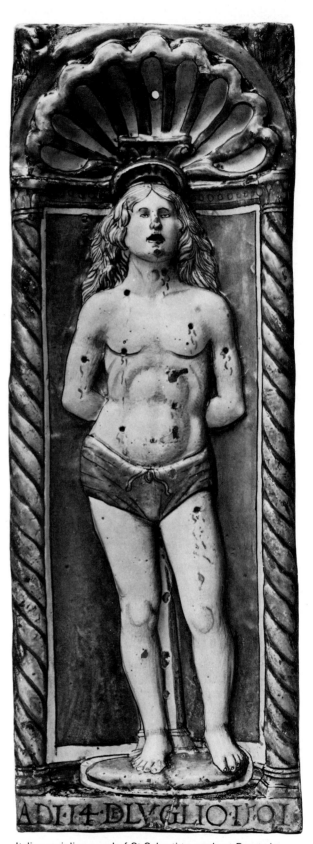

Italian maiolica panel of St Sebastian, made at Deruta in 1501. A very early example of the lustre technique

from the tin-enamel itself. There was also the lustre technique, imported from Spain, and used principally at Gubbio and Deruta.

So much for techniques, but Renaissance maiolica brought something new to the art of pottery. Firstly, there was a love of display: a desire to have everything not only as beautiful but as lavish as possible, and almost for the first time, a desire to collect. Secondly, the new belief in man as an intrinsically important being; this made reasonable the making of individual pieces of pottery. These were not necessarily for use—each one was a unique creation and valued as such. This brings us to the third point: the inter-relationship of the arts during the Renaissance. In the Middle Ages, pottery had come very low in the hierarchy of the arts, but when almost all the great men of the Renaissance interested themselves in several arts at once, this scheme of things was bound to change. Pottery came into closer contact than it ever had before with the other arts, such as painting and the graphic arts, sculpture and metalwork. The influence of painting and engraving on maiolica is especially apparent. If the new status of ceramics in Italy could be attributed to one man, he was Luca

Italian Medici porcelain bottle, made in Florence about 1580

Italian maiolica plate with Leda and the Swan, made by Jacopo Fattorini at Cafaggiolo, about 1515

della Robbia. Primarily he remained a sculptor, but by using maiolica techniques to give his work colour as well as form, he at the same time inspired the potters (especially the potters of Faenza) to a new freedom of expression.

In France the earliest wares using the tin-enamel glaze, those of Bernard Palissy, were very much akin to della Robbia's work, but Palissy's reptilian creatures that swarm in his dishes have a nastiness all their own.

More innocent is English delft. Really the name 'delft' is a misnomer, because the English began making these wares long before the Dutch did. It would make better sense to call the pottery made in Holland 'Dutch Lambeth' or some such term. But even in England, the technique was not developed until the very end of the sixteenth century.

French faïence Palissy ware
dish with animals moulded in
high relief and coloured in
lead-glazes. Second half of
the 16th century

Below English delft dish,
1600. The design in the
centre represents the
Tower of London

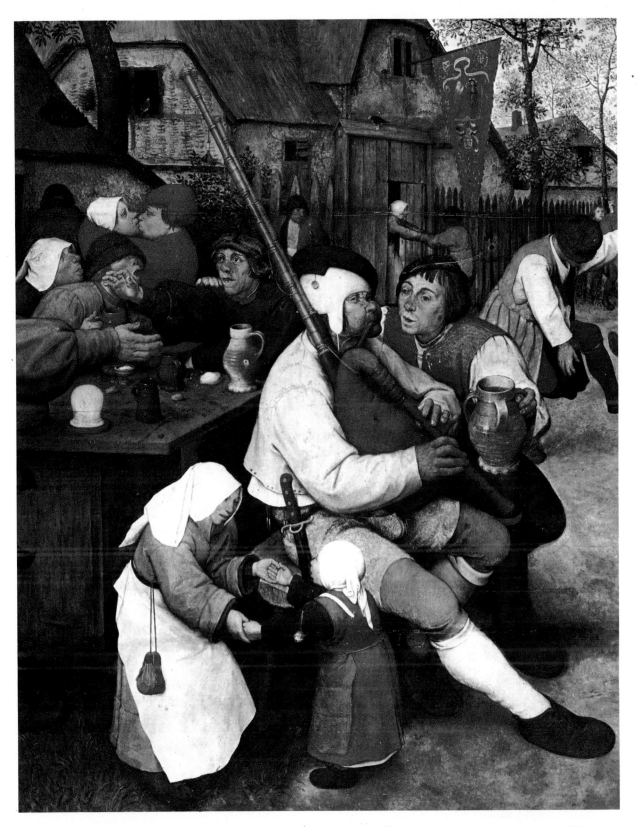

Detail from 'The Peasant Dance by Bruegel, about 1567, showing jugs and mugs in everyday use

The sixteenth century

Italian maiolica dish, made at Faenza about 1525. The figure of Lucretia is based on Marcantonio Raimondi's engraving of a work by Raphael

The sixteenth century also saw the earliest European experiments in making porcelain. The passion for it goes back to Marco Polo (thirteenth century) and so does the name. The Chinese called it 'yao'; Marco Polo, speaking in metaphor, used the word 'porcelain' (which meant a shell) to try to convey the translucency of the material. The name caught on, and the sea-shell idea persisted long after that. A certain Italian lawyer of the sixteenth century, Guido Panciroli, wrote in his *Brief Account of Certain Excellent things known to the Ancients* that porcelain is **a substance made of chalk, pounded egg, and shells of sea-locusts, pressed together with other similar things and hidden underground by the maker, who tells none but his children and his grandchildren where it is. And they, eighty years later, dig it out and shape it into beautiful vases.**

Not very promising as a recipe, this passage indicates nevertheless the mysterious quality that porcelain was felt to have. It was, for instance, supposed to be effective in warding off illnesses and protecting against poisoning; consequently, perhaps, it was a favourite gift for the royalty and aristocracy.

It was in Italy that experiments began. The versatile Bernardo Buontalenti, 'a man of brilliant talent, who can turn his hand to anything', began to make for the Medici court in Florence pieces from a yellowish paste derived from the

so-called white clay of Vicenza. These he covered with a white glaze; this was Medici porcelain, the earliest porcelain to be made in Europe. Examples of this ware are, however, very rare indeed – and consequently prohibitively expensive – for only a few pieces were made before the Grand-Duke Francesco, who had financed the enterprise, died in 1587. That put an end to the experiments, until they were resumed in other countries in the following century.

Silver

The discovery and subsequent exploitation of the Americas, and in particular of Mexico and Peru, brought new wealth to Europe. Such *conquistadores* as Cortes and Pizarro obtained, often by violent and unscrupulous means, quantities of bullion, both gold and silver. There was more scope for work in precious metals in the sixteenth century than there had been previously; a new lavishness became possible.

Whereas in the Middle Ages, France had been the principal centre for work in gold and silver, the focus now shifted to Italy, Rome and Florence especially. Had much work in these metals survived from classical antiquity, no doubt Italian Renaissance craftsmen would have used this as a source of design. Since in fact very little did, they turned rather to ancient sculpture and architecture; the casket made by Valerio Belli for presentation by Pope Clement VII to François I of France clearly illustrates this. But

Spanish circular salver of embossed and chased silver-gilt. Early 16th century

24

German columbine-shaped cup, made at Nuremberg, about 1590. Dürer's home town was famed for its metalwork

the great virtue of Italian Renaissance silver is not its antiquarianism, but its new fluidity of design. Probably the supreme example is the magnificent salt made, again for François I, by Benvenuto Cellini in 1543. One tends to look on this piece rather as sculpture. One forgets that the boat-shaped vessel on one side should in fact hold the salt and the small Ionic temple on the other the pepper, so entirely are they dominated by the figures of Neptune the god of the sea and Tellus the goddess of the earth.

Salts had a special significance in the sixteenth century. Modern cruets are just receptacles for condiments, but the salt was the centrepiece of the table. If one sat above the salt, that is at the master's end of the table, one was a member of the élite; if one sat below it, one was no more than a hanger-on. So the great salt was generally the most splendid piece of plate the household possessed; this applied throughout Europe, in England (for example, the Gibbon Salt) as in Italy. But there was one item that the Italian nobleman might possess which was quite unknown elsewhere: a fork..

Thomas Coryat notes in *Coryats Crudities* how the Italians **do always at their meals use a little fork when they cut their meat . . . their forks being for the most part made of iron or steel, and some of silver, but those are used only by gentlemen. The reason of this their curiosity is, because the Italian cannot by any means endure to have his dish touched with fingers, seeing all mens' fingers are not alike clean. . . .**

The Vyvyan Salt, English, silver-gilt, 1592–3

Designs for six goblets: pen drawing by Albrecht Dürer

Opposite page The Gibbon Salt: a silver-gilt salt of architectural design made in London, 1576

Left German clock, gilt copper with enamelled silver panels. The clock face is set horizontally. Augsburg, Germany·16th century

Below The François I gold salt, made by Benvenuto Cellini. The two main figures represent Tellus (Earth) and Neptune (Sea). The miniature Ionic temple is for pepper and a boat-shaped vessel for salt. Begun in Rome in 1540, completed in France

The sixteenth century

Coryat was much impressed with this custom, and decided to adopt it himself.

The Italians led the way in design as well as in hygiene, and the art of the silversmith prospered. In other countries, too, north of the Alps, artists did not feel they were demeaning themselves if they designed work in precious metals. We have from Dürer's hand drawings of this kind, and from Holbein's an actual cup and cover, made in London, of rock crystal, gold and jewels.

Although the Renaissance style in silver was widely adopted, there were national differences. The Spanish, for instance, were fond of all-over patterning, possibly Islamic in origin. The Germans liked intricacy, and produced many tall standing cups, often with bell-shaped bowls and repoussé moulding – that is to say, with protruberances pushed out from the inside. Such pieces were for display, or done as test-pieces for admission to a guild; they had no practical use.

Glass

The basic requirements for glass are silica, alkali and fuel. Even more vital is the knowledge of how to use these materials. The Egyptians were, as far as we know, the first to discover the art of glass-making. Then under the Romans, but mainly in Syria and Alexandria, it was developed to a very fine art indeed. After the Roman Empire fell, the skill seems to have been lost in Italy, at least by the fifth century, although in Gaul it apparently lingered rather longer, and after that itinerant glass-makers continued to move around Europe.

In Syria, however, it appears that the art of glass-making never died out, and it was through Venetian merchants trading with the Middle East that it was decisively re-introduced into Europe. By the thirteenth century, there was already a thriving glass industry in Venice, but by the sixteenth century, Venetian glass was at the zenith of its achievement and Venice had replaced Syria as a world centre of glass-making. Silica they obtained from the white pebbles of the rivers Po and Ticino; the alkali came from soda-ash from certain marine plants. To this was added powdered marble or crushed sea-shells, to increase the lime content. From the end of the thirteenth century onwards, Venetian glass was made not in the city itself (because of the risk of fires being caused by the furnaces) but on the island of Murano. This helped, moreover,

German pilgrim's bottle in enamelled glass, dating from after 1530

to guard the secrets of glass-making from inquisitive foreigners.

Foreigners were certainly inquisitive, because Venetian glass was very much in vogue. William Harrison wrote in his 'Description of England', **It is a world to see in these our days, wherein gold and silver most aboundeth, how that our gentry, as loathing those metals because of their plenty, do not generally choose rather the Venice glasses, both for our wine and beer, than any of those metals or stone wherein beforetime we have been accustomed to drink. And as this is seen in the gentility, so in the wealthy communalty the like desire of glass is not neglected. The poorest also will have their glass if they may, but, sith the Venetian is somewhat too dear for them, they content themselves with such as are made at home of fern and burned stone.**

The Venetians made clear glass—not always very clear in our eyes because soda-glass seldom is. Sometimes they decorated it with gilding or enamelling—the enamel was frequently applied simply as coloured spots, a technique known as 'gemming'. The glass was extremely thin and fragile, so it was seldom cut or engraved; it was, however, sometimes decorated with mouldings. The Venetians also experimented with 'lattimo' (opaque white or milk-glass), 'millefiori' (literally, a thousand flowers), and glass which imitated jasper, chalcedony, lapis-lazuli and tortoise-shell. In the sixteenth century, they developed very delicate hollow-stem glasses, often decorated with a pair of lion masks, or fantastic ornaments in coloured glass, commonly blue, either side of the stem.

Above Venetian wine-glass in colourless and blue glass. 16th century

Right Venetian wine-glass, semi-transparent with spiral mouldings: 16th century

Glass goblet diamond-engraved "John-Jone, Dier" by Verzelini, 1581

Early German glass was largely developed from the Venetian. Characteristic decoration included what in Germany were called 'Nuppen' and in England 'raspberry prunts', small knobbly seals attached to the outer surface. Enamelled glass was also much in favour; marriages were commemorated with glasses enamelled with the coats of arms of the two families.

In England, an Italian glass-maker called Giacomo Verzelini was in 1575 granted sole right to make Venetian glass for the next twenty-one years, and no glass was permitted to be imported from Venice. The earliest dated specimen of Verzelini glass, from 1577, is in the Steuben Collection, New York. The Verzelini glasses are diamond-engraved, possibly by one Anthony de Lysle, a pewter and glass engraver said to be of French origin.

The Double Cube Room, Wilton House, Wiltshire, England.
Built about 1640, its design and decoration were planned by
Inigo Jones

Detail of Grinling Gibbons' carving at Petworth House: a
group of musical instruments including violin, kit, and
recorder, with sheet music, oak and olive branches, lace,
quiver and chaplet with portrait

The Heaven Room at Burghley House, Northamptonshire.
The 'trompre-l'œil' decoration was painted by Antonio Verrio
about 1696

The seventeenth century

When Galileo discovered in 1610 that the earth was not, after all, the centre of the universe, men's sense of order was shattered.

And new Philosophy calls all in doubt,
The element of fire is quite put out;
The sun is lost, and th'earth, and no man's wit
Can direct him where to look for it.

So wrote John Donne in his 'Anatomy of the World'. Having lost the sun, he could no longer speak optimistically about the earth he lived on:

For the world's beauty is decayed, or gone,
Beauty, that's colour and proportion.

And if the earth was not central to the universe, how could man believe—as he had in Renaissance times—that he himself occupied a central position in the scheme of things? His stature

The King's Bedroom, Knole, Sevenoaks, Kent, England, showing silver furniture and Mortlake tapestries. This room is supposed to have been prepared for the reception of King James I, but most of the furnishings are of later 17th-century date

was diminished. His body, he felt, was no more than a heavy weight his soul had to drag around with it, and as for infinity, in Pascal's words, 'the eternal silence of those limitless spaces terrifies me'.

As the century wore on, man began to search for new harmonies, new proportions, a chart for those limitless spaces and some order in all this apparent chaos. He found it within himself. He realised that what distinguished him from the rest of creation, what made him something more than worm-fodder, was the power of thought. 'I think, therefore I am', declared Descartes. 'Man is nothing but a reed, the feeblest thing in nature', wrote Pascal, 'but he is a thinking reed.'

The philosophers' search for new harmonies was reflected in the arts. After all, men's hands do not work independently from their minds. So arose the style which we call 'baroque'.

No seventeenth-century artist would have recognised this word as one that had anything to do with the arts. The term 'baroque' was derived from the Portuguese word 'barroco' which meant a pearl of irregular shape. 'Baroque' was used, though not until well on into the eighteenth century, to signify inperfect or misshapen; it was a term of abuse. The eighteenth century condemned the prevailing style of the seventeenth, because it was felt that there could be no rightness in what seemed a departure from classical regularity. What they could not perceive as harmony they accounted discord. 'Baroque is the ultimate in the bizarre, it is the ridiculous carried to extremes' wrote the Italian critic Milizia in 1797, and it was not

Louis XIV and his heirs: painting by N. Largillière. Behind the duchesse de Ventadour (the little duc de Bretagne's governess) stands a vase either of Chinese origin or of soft paste porcelain from Rouen or St Cloud

The seventeenth century

until much later that the word lost this contemptuous flavour. We now realise that art in the seventeenth century was not just anarchy, whim and a blind disregard for the proper rules. Baroque artists were in fact searching for a new order. They realised that, while harmony had certainly been found in that perfect circle which may be said to express the Renaissance ideal, it could also be seen in the ellipse; for example, in the oval salon at Vaux-le-Vicomte. There was harmony in balance as well as in symmetry, in movement as well as in stillness.

Baroque artists approached their work with these ideas in mind. They brought to it a new dynamism, new sense of theatre and yet at the same time a new sense of involvement – the expression of violent emotions was no longer considered improper in a work of art, they could now be given full rein. There was a fine exuberance of forms and a preference for open-ended compositions; and yet in the midst of all this movement there was a search for pattern, not for centrality but for counterpoise.

Baroque art is also characterized by its use of rich colour, its warmth, its new sensuousness. If we look at a baroque interior, for instance the Heaven Room at Burghley House, these are the qualities we notice. But the style began not in domestic interiors but in churches, in the churches of Rome, particularly the new Jesuit churches being built under the impulse of the Counter-Reformation. It was an expression of faith; it was all done to the greater glory of God and his saints.

The Oval Salon at Vaux-le-Vicomte, France, designed by
Le Vau, begun 1657

One would not expect artists in Protestant countries to express themselves in this way. The saints were of small account and the making of their images had ceased. The art which grew up in such countries as Holland was, therefore, almost entirely secular, and had far more affinity with science than with religion. One has to say 'almost' because there was one important exception, the greatest figure in all Dutch art, Rembrandt. His intensely personal religious convictions are an integral part of his work. But if we look at a painting by Vermeer, we find a realism, a clarity of light and vision, a stillness even, which is more classical than baroque. Yet the Dutch minor arts are far more full of exuberant forms than one might have expected, silver especially, as is evident from the splendidly ornate jug in the still life by Willem Kalf.

It is not far-fetched to draw a parallel with architecture in England. Inigo Jones (who was, incidentally, this country's first professional architect) wrote: **for as outwardly every wise man carrieth a gravity in Publicke Places, where there is nothing else to be looked for, yet inwardly hath his immaginacy set on fire . . . so in architecture ye outward ornaments ought to be solid, proportionable according to the rules, masculine and unaffected.** Plainness and decorum he recommended for large works and interiors; yet within, and in little things, fancy could run riot. So we find his Double Cube Room at Wilton House near Salisbury based on a rigid mathematical formula, yet quite a degree of exciting detail within it. The Grinling Gibbons carvings at Petworth House, Sussex, would no doubt have won his approval, because their intricacy and naturalism were confined to decorating an interior.

Still-life with jug and fruit by Willem Kalf, about 1660. The jug is Dutch baroque silver, the intricate glass probably Venetian, and the fruit bowl possibly a delft imitation of Chinese porcelain

Carved and gilded bed, English, early 17th century. The hangings are green velvet. Venetian Ambassador's Bedroom, Knole, Sevenoaks, Kent, England

The seventeenth century

While England compromised, France under Louis XIV saw an outright revival of classicism. Louis XIV was an extraordinarily self-opinionated man, who believed himself at least semi-divine. Calling himself the Sun King, he held a ritual levée and couchée as he got up and went to bed. Courtiers thought themselves greatly honoured when they were asked to do the most menial tasks for him. Constantly he liked to celebrate his power and magnificence with festivals and spectacles. He established his court at Versailles. He encouraged all the arts, he established academies. Versailles became the pattern for all other courts. Yet in all this cultural splendour there was a trend towards regimentation: a trend which in literature was expressed in the Académie's attempts to fossilize the language, and in the visual arts in a rigorous classicism—also in the superhuman scale of such a place as Versailles; it seems to have been built for someone much larger than life.

Below This late 17th-century print, attributed to Francis Place, shows the interior of the Octagon Room, Old Royal Observatory, Greenwich England, designed by Sir Christopher Wren. The clock shown on the left is one of two made by Thomas Tompion for this setting in 1676

CAMERAM STELLATAM.

Family Group, by Hieronymus Janssens of Antwerp.
See page 39

The seventeenth century, although full of contrasts and at times politically stormy, was in general a period of material prosperity. It was a time when even philosophers felt they could come out of retreat and find stimulus in a social urban existence. This is Descartes, in a letter to Guez de Balzac, 1631, enthusing about Amsterdam: **You must excuse my zeal if I invite you to choose Amsterdam for your retirement, and to prefer it to all the Capuchin and Carthusian monasteries, to which many worthy people retire, but also to the finest residences in France and Italy, and even to the famous hermitage where you lived last year. However well organized a house in the country may be, it always lacks an infinite number of commodities which can be found only in towns, while even the solitude one hopes to find there is never complete... No doubt there is a pleasure to be derived from watching the fruit in your orchards grow in great abundance, but do you imagine one cannot see at least as much here in Amsterdam, unloaded by the vessels that bring us such a copious supply of everything produced in the Indies and all that is rare in Europe? Which other place in the whole world could one choose where all the commodities of life are so easy to find as in Amsterdam?**

Amongst these commodities were works of art of all kinds, and much to tempt the collector. Rembrandt himself acquired a fine array of Venetian glass, oriental porcelain and fans, splendid helmets and shields, as well as paintings, etchings and engravings. The sterner philosophers might scoff as Bacon did: 'Antiquities are history defaced, or some remnants of history which have casually escaped the shipwreck of time' (*Advancement of Learning*, 1605). Solemn Spanish court painters like Antonio Palomino might dismiss applied art as 'contemptible or sordid because it stains, lowers and defiles the excellence of the individual's rank and person' (*Pictorial Museum and Optical Scale*). But there was no doubt about it; fine things were being made and so were collections.

The seventeenth century

Furniture

This was a period when a growing desire for comfort gradually gave way to a passion for pomp. Like most generalizations, this is not entirely true. In Italy, the process was rather the other way round. Italy was the cradle of the baroque style in architecture and sculpture, and furniture design at the beginning of the century was almost an extension of these arts. Horizontals were supported by putti and caryatids, dolphins and eagles; there was much carving and gilding, some use of semi-precious stone or 'pietra dura' decoration. Little of what a purist would consider real cabinet-making, but it was all very opulent and sculpturesque and reflected the great wealth of certain merchant families, who vied with each other in the splendour of their palaces.

The Renaissance *cassone* was now outmoded and the wardrobe took its place. There were richly ornate cabinets, and heavy ornamental tables and console tables (these were an innovation), more or less based on classical predecessors. Chairs were often equally elaborate: the craftsman most famous for these was Andrea Brustolon, who worked largely in Venice and was typical of this style in being more of a sculptor than a cabinet-maker.

In France, meanwhile, there was a gradual revival of all the arts under Henri IV, until that king's unexpected assassination in 1610. Then the Italian influence came in through his widow Marie de Medicis during the reign of her son Louis XIII: a love of gilt, stucco and inlaid work; and Italian craftsmen were imported so that this taste might be indulged. Cabinets were the new showpieces. At first they too were imported from Italy, Germany and Flanders. As in Italy, the wardrobe or *armoire* was developed; armchairs became lower in the seat and, with their padded backs and curved arms, more comfortable. A more truly French taste asserted itself in the reign of Louis XIV. In 1661, at the age of

17th Century French cabinet. The upper stage may be by A C Boulle; the supporting figures of Summer (left) and Autumn (right) are of later date

French armchair, Louis XIV period. The arms are carved with acanthus leaves

twenty-three, he took over the government and simultaneously gave great encouragement to the arts. Given a lead by Nicolas Fouquet, his minister of finance (who had established workshops at Maincy in order to furnish Vaux-le-Vicomte), Louis acquired the premises of the Gobelins brothers on the outskirts of Paris, and set up workshops there not only for tapestries but for all the applied arts. These he put under the general control of the painter Charles le Brun, and the establishment was known as 'La Manufacture Royale des Meubles de la Couronne'. The whole purpose was to add to the splendour of Versailles, the new palace he was creating around his father's old hunting-lodge.

The furniture made for Versailles was monumental in its classicism until the Roman manner was given a new gaiety and vitality through the designs of Jean Berain. While the Gobelins workshops were temporarily closed (1694–1697), perhaps the greatest of the century's furniture-makers rose into prominence, André-Charles Boulle (1642–1732). His name is associated with a type of inlaid decoration he popularised, using tortoise-shell and brass. Other veneering techniques were used, using laburnum, holly, sycamore, pearwood; oriental lacquer was also favoured.

Of taste in Flanders we can get a fair idea from the family group by Janssens. Lit by the same high windows as were common in Holland, there is a rectangular massing of pictures and furniture. Most of the furniture is heavy. The cabinet at the back with its painted wings and architectural interior is obviously a show-piece. Characteristic of the time are the great barley-sugar twisting columns on the right of the picture (ultimately derived perhaps from Bernini's stupendous baldacchino in St Peter's, Rome). The general impression is one of self-conscious aspiration to culture.

American mushroom-armed great chair, late 17th century

English silver table, 1680–81, and silver-framed mirror. Knole, Sevenoaks, Kent, England

Carving by Grinling Gibbons, from Petworth House, Sussex, England. About 1690

The seventeenth century

Cabinets, exquisitely inlaid, which inside are like pieces of architecture in miniature, were the speciality of Antwerp and south Germany. Their interiors perhaps most closely resemble the architectural *frons scaenae* (stage arches) and clever perspectives of the Italian theatre – Palladio's Teatro Olimpico at Vicenza, for instance. In any case, these cabinets were prize pieces, made for show, not for use. In the same category come the so-called dolls' houses from Germany and Holland; they were never intended for

in the Royal Collection and at Knole House, Sevenoaks, Kent. More common were Asiatic lacquered wares which came by way of the East India Company. The Restoration period saw the development of marquetry (veneers cut from different woods fixed to a solid carcase – parquetry is the same thing but uses geometric designs) and a new flowering in carved decoration. The best-known exponent of this was Grinling Gibbons (1648–1720). Originally a ship-carver, he was discovered by the diarist

Antwerp or South German inlaid cabinet, mid-17th century. The 'stage-set' interior was probably based on theatre design, such as the Teatro Olimpico, Vicenza **right**

children to play with.

English furniture of the early seventeenth century is little changed from Elizabethan. In fact, the full-blooded baroque style never really caught on. There were some innovations: more chairs were made with upholstered seats and some, which were called back-stools, without arms. Gate-leg tables became common, the first chests of drawers were made. Only occasionally was anything made as splendid and elaborate as the Venetian Ambassador's bed at Knole. More often furniture was solid, four-square and, during the Commonwealth period, remarkably plain. The simplicity and solidity of American seventeenth-century furniture is a legacy of this Puritan taste.

Only after the restoration of the monarchy in 1660 did English furniture show much affinity with continental design. The new king, Charles II, brought in, so writes John Evelyn in his diary, 'a politer way of living which soon passed to luxury and intolerable expense.' As an exile he had learnt something of French taste. Silver furniture, such as was made for Versailles (but melted down in the eighteenth century), survives

Dutch 'doll's house', walnut, about 1700

Evelyn in a humble cottage in Deptford, and introduced to the court. Gibbons preferred to leave the natural colour and grain of the wood, rather than gild it or paint it. One of his finest achievements is the Carved Room at Petworth House, which Walpole described as 'gloriously flounced all round . . . there are birds absolutely feathered: and two antique vases with bas-reliefs, as perfect and beautiful as if they were carved by a Grecian master.'

Ceramics

The seventeenth century was primarily a period for earthenware, secondarily for stoneware, and not at all for porcelain. Stoneware is a type of pottery made from the simple basic material, clay, but fixed at white heat ($1250°-1350°$C) until it is fused and vitrified; even without glaze it is impervious to moisture. Porcelain has been defined on page 24.

In France, the potters were at first much influenced by the Italian maiolica of the Renaissance. The first important French centre was at Nevers. There they used sometimes a white ground with blue decoration, and sometimes a

German glass 'Humpen', enamelled with drinking scenes. 1609

English delft charger, showing Charles I and three of his children. Dated 1653

deep blue ground peculiar to this pottery. This blue ground was called, mistakenly, 'bleu persan' by the first director of the Sèvres Museum—he thought the ware was Persian—and the name has stuck. The blue ground was painted with designs in white alone, or with white, orange and yellow.

At the same time a factory at Rouen had been

opened in 1647, and enjoyed a monoply throughout Normandy for fifty years. Although it never had a royal patent, this pottery supplied all the tiles and vases for the Trianon de Porcelaine commissioned by Louis XIV in 1670; and as a source of inspiration it drew largely on the other applied arts made for Versailles—embroidery, gold and silver, and wrought-ironwork. Sometimes there was a hint of pseudo-Chinese influence, sometimes it adopted the symmetrical, almost geometrical type of design known as the 'style rayonnant'.

In Holland, Delft pottery developed much at the same time as French faïence. The origin of the name is clear enough; though the Dutch themselves sometimes call it 'porseleyne'. This is confusing, but significant; for much of it was done in imitation of Chinese porcelain. The Dutch East India Company brought in quantities of Chinese porcelain which, since it was understandably expensive, the potters in Holland did their best to copy.

English delft was made throughout the century. These early delftwares are from London (Lambeth). The other important centres at Bristol and Liverpool developed later. At first, the whole colour-range possible was not fully realised. Then the greens, blues and yellows developed and brightened. 'Blue dash' chargers were made, so called because of their border decoration; some of the most delightful chargers are painted with crude but lively portrayals of the reigning monarch or even royal family groups–the best, and the rarest, are the earlier ones.

English slipware dish by Thomas Toft of Staffordshire. Second half 17th century

French faience flask (pilgrim-bottle) from Nevers, decorated in cobalt with Persian-inspired figures

Other English earthenware, which we should not call delft, was decorated with 'slip'. Slip is a mixture of clay and water and can be used either in place of a coloured glaze (it is not in itself glossy, so a transparent glaze has to be applied afterwards), or trailed on like icing from an icing-gun. It was first used at Wrotham in Kent in the early seventeenth century, but much more famous are the wares made in Staffordshire later in the century by the Toft family; Thomas Toft seems to have been the most skilled of them.

Stoneware began as a German speciality. German stoneware, or 'Steinzeug', was made principally in the Westerwald and at Cologne, Sieburg and Raeren; it varies in colour from white at Sieburg to bluish-grey in the Westerwald. Usually it was salt-glazed and has a slightly pitted surface, like orange-skin. Seventeenth-century examples often have overglaze designs in enamels. This is the first time enamels were used to decorate European ceramics. Possibly, the technique was borrowed from Bohemian glass.

German stoneware 'Humpen' tankard, made in Kreussen, 1627, decorated with sun, moon and planets

In Britain, stoneware was made from the second half of the century onwards, but the first name we meet is that of John Dwight of Fulham, who obtained in 1671 a patent for the 'mistery of transparent earthenware, commonly known as porcelaine or china, and of stoneware, vulgarly called Cologne ware' (there seems to have been some confusion over the nomenclature). His only serious rivals were the Elers brothers, originally silversmiths, who worked in Staffordshire and made a fine brick-red stoneware.

Dwight produced bottles and jars in the German manner; and also made busts and figures—which are astonishing achievements when one considers the crudity of the material and the high temperature at which it was fired. Perhaps the most touching of these—with its little pinched-up face—is the memorial to his daughter Lydia, who died very young in 1673.

English salt-glazed stoneware by John Dwight: memorial for his daughter Lydia. Inscribed on back 'Lydia Dwight dyed March 3 1673'

Dutch delftware: the vase imitates a Chinese shape and decoration, and the jug shows a vase of this type in the background of a room

Silver

The peace and prosperity of a country is often reflected in its silver, which ceases to be produced when times are hard. In fact, what is already in existence is melted down in order to settle some urgent account. Our predecessors might have thought twice about melting down a large and highly wrought piece, but a few odd spoons were too easy to turn into currency, which is why so few small pieces of early silver survive today. And what we might now treasure as an antique, they discarded as old-fashioned.

Forks were still a rarity in any case, though from the 1630s onwards they are occasionally to be found from countries other than Italy, where they had originated. By the end of the century, sets of knife, fork and spoon were commonly made, sometimes ornate, sometimes strictly practical for travelling, for it was quite usual to carry one's own set with one.

As the fortunes of a country fluctuated, so did its production of silver. At the beginning of the century, Germany was in the forefront, and the main centres were Augsburg and Nuremberg. Fashions were slow to change; for instance, the Augsburg cup and cover now in the Wallace Collection is still very much in the Renaissance tradition. Various tankards and cups and

Dutch mirror, framed in delft earthenware with scrolls, virtues, amorini, shell and leaf design

The seventeenth century

beakers were made: typically German was the 'pineapple' cup, the repoussé protruberances on which bear some resemblance to that fruit. With the disasters of the Thirty Years War, Germany declined as a centre for silver, and Holland took her place, retaining her supremacy right up to the time of Louis XIV. Dutch silversmiths excelled in repoussé work, but what is so surprising, considering the reticence of form characteristic of most of the arts in Holland, is the wonderfully free Baroque design of their silver. It is as though they reserved this one art for the casting off of all their inhibitions. Dutch silver design was led by the van Vianen family: first Paul, then his brother Adam, then Adam's son Christiaan, produced courageously asymmetrical pieces with flowing lines, frequently incorporating human, plant and animal forms. The van Vianen baroque style was continued and developed by Johannes Lutma, who worked in Amsterdam around the middle of the century.

At just about the time when Lutma died in 1669, the French took the lead in silver design. It is not surprising that Louis XIV found this medium a suitable one to express his self-aggrandisement. The patronage of king and court at Versailles rapidly transformed the art. Very beautiful and elaborate pieces were made - much of it, unfortunately, only to be melted

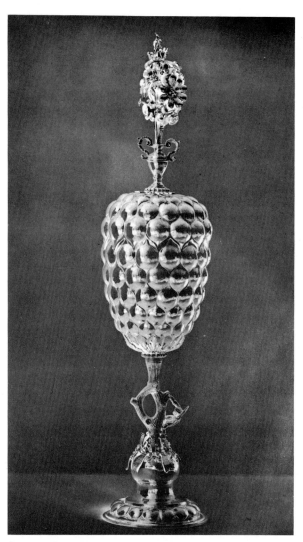

German silver-gilt pineapple cup and cover. Nuremberg, about 1615

Augsburg cup and cover, silver and silver-gilt, with arabesques of enamel. About 1600

Dutch silver dish with Apollo and Daphne, by Adam van Vianen, 1620

44

Huguenots, including craftsmen of all kinds, fled from persecution in their own country, and numbers of them settled in England. Some of the English smiths resented this as an intrusion. Technically, the Huguenots' work was far in advance of theirs, which was perhaps why.

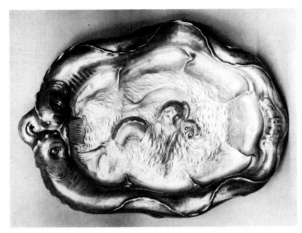

Dutch silver: large dish with dolphins, by Christiaan van Vianen, 1635

Silver casket from the Lennoxlove Toilet Service, dating between 1661 and 1667

down when Louis needed money for his campaigns. The famous Lennoxlove toilet service, made in Paris in 1672–1677 by Pierre Flamand for presentation by Charles II to the Duchess of Richmond and Lennoxlove, probably only survived because it was exported to Britain.

As for British silver, the preference during the early years of the century was for simple design, much less ornate than contemporary German. By 1630, even entirely plain plate was commonly made. During the Commonwealth, little silver was made and the London silversmiths were unemployed, so what little there was tends to be of a provincial nature. With the Reformation, there was some influence of Dutch taste and even more of French. Charles II imported silversmiths from France, where he had spent his years of exile. Then in 1666,

English silver wine cup, 1617

The seventeenth century

Glass

At the beginning of the century, glass-making was still dominated by Venice. Venetian glass continued very much in vogue all over Europe. A new decorative device was now used, *vitro di trina* or lace glass: the clear glass was patterned with threads of opaque white glass until the general effect was rather like lace. Venetian glass was often blown until it was quite thin in section and the thinness helped to disguise the fact that the actual body or 'metal' of the glass was greyish, with a tendency to bubbles. Much was made for export. Towards the end of the century Venetian glass declined as the workers of Murano were lured away to work elsewhere. At the same time, glass in the Venetian manner

was being made in Belgium (Antwerp and Liège), France (Lorraine) and England. Around 1670, a certain John Greene of the English Glass Sellers Company was designing glass which was made by Alessio Morelli in Murano: English glass, made in Venice.

In Germany and Bohemia, and also in Barcelona in Spain, there was a fashion for enamelled wares. This is more than simply painting; the decoration has to be fired to make it permanent, and a precise control of temperature is necessary. The characteristically German shapes, frequently enamelled, were 'Passgläser' (banded glasses) and 'Humpen' (lidded jars). In the late seventeenth-century coloured glass, especially 'ruby', was made in Potsdam.

While some glass was made in Holland, particularly at The Hague and Maastricht, a general lack of fuel (the Dutch had no coal as an alternative to wood) limited its manufacture. Therefore the Dutch specialised in engraving

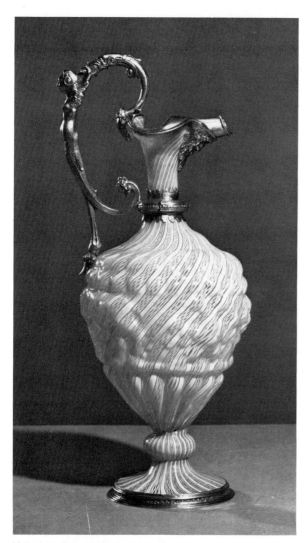

Venetian glass ewer with 'lace glass' decoration: silver-gilt mount with Nuremberg hallmark. Early 17th century

Dutch engraved glass 'Roemer' by Anna Roemers Visscher, 1621

imported glass. They employed the techniques of diamond-engraving and, later, wheel-engraving to such effect that they were unrivalled in these skills.

In the early years of the seventeenth century, English glass-making was monopolised by one man, Sir Robert Mansell. He brought in coal from Scotland to stoke his furnaces. We know that Mansell was not a craftsman but a businessman – and a ruthless one at that – but virtually no Mansell glass survives, so we cannot judge its quality. His monopoly seems to have continued until the beginning of the Civil War. After the Restoration, the Glass Sellers' Company received its charter and for fourteen years the making of glass was very largely financed by George Villiers, Duke of Buckingham. To all the leading glassmakers he paid salaries and secured the patents for himself. The Royal Oak goblet, made to commemorate the marriage of Charles II with Catherine of Braganza, is the most celebrated glass to survive from the Duke's factories.

In 1673, George Ravenscroft built a glasshouse at the Savoy in London, and there he developed a new metal which combined strength with clarity: nowhere in Europe was there anything to touch the quality of Ravenscroft glass. His technique was to add lead oxide. It was not perfected until 1685, but from 1677 his glasses bear the 'raven's head' seal as his mark. Ravenscroft put England in the forefront of European glass-making, and there she was to stay for the next hundred years.

Another view of the 'Roemer' on page 46

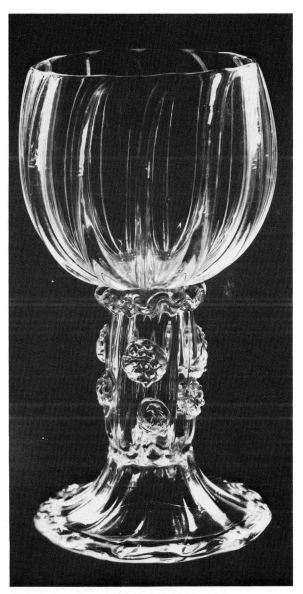

English glass: Ravenscroft 'Roemer' with raven's head seal, about 1677

From left to right
German fork, 16th century
French knife, chiselled and gilt, 16th century
English knife, fork and spoon, London 1692–3

Dutch silver spoon, 1713

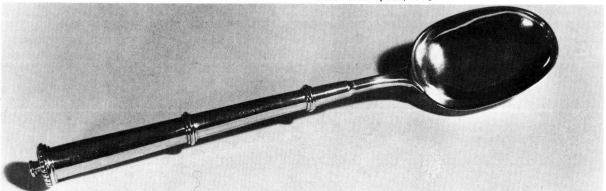

From left to right
Silver serving spoon, Exeter, 1726
Penknife, Sheffield, late 18th century
Strainer spoon, London, 1791
Knife, ivory handle with silver mounts, Sheffield, about 1800

Knives, *when pointed, were used for spearing as well as for cutting meat.* **Forks** *were still a rarity in the 16th century, but by the 17th century it was considered polite to carry one's own set of cutlery,* *often in a leather case.* **Spoons** *were becoming generally more pointed and less oval in shape.* **Penknives** *were used for cutting quill pens*

Above French wardrobe by A. C. Boulle, veneered on oak, with ebony and marquetry of brass and tortoise-shell. The main decorative panel on the left shows Apollo and Daphne, that on the right the Flaying of Marsyas

Opposite page English cabinet incorporating Chinese lacquered panels, about 1685

Above Italian harpsichord, made in Venice by Giovanni Baffo, 1574

Below German 'positive organ,' probably by Gottfried Fritsche, 1627

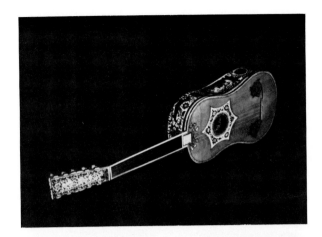

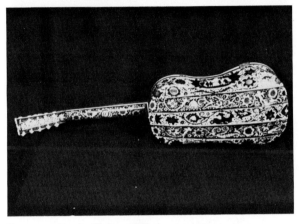

German guitar, by Tielke, 1693: front and back views

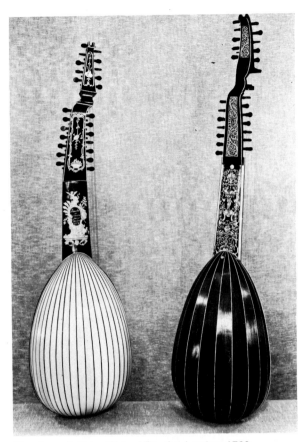

Theorboes: **left** by Michael Rauche, London, 1762, **right** by J H Goldt, Hamburg, 1734

English violin, ornamented with the arms of the House of Stuart; last third of the 17th century

French pedal-harp by H. Nadermann, Paris, about 1785

German bass viol, by Martin Voigt, Hamburg, 1726

Right Detail from 'The Music Lesson', painting by Jan Vermeer of Delft. Besides the musical instruments, this Dutch interior shows a 'Turkey' carpet and white earthenware ewer, both probably made in Delft

Above French faïence jug, 'bleu persan' ware from Nevers, late 17th century

1700–1750

Curiously the prevailing feeling in the early eighteenth century was one of optimism. While this did not happen overnight, there was a sense that the old doubts and fears had been dismissed and a new dawn was breaking.

Nature and Nature's laws lay hid in night:
God said, Let Newton be! and all was light!

wrote Alexander Pope. It was no mystic awakening, but men such as Pope claimed to see a new pattern in creation. They looked at the world around them; while a few were living in luxury, a few more in comparative comfort, yet it could not be denied that there was Gin Lane, that twelve-year-olds were set to work long hours in the mines, small boys were sent up chimneys to clean them, and the infant mortality rate was what we should call appalling. For instance, in London during a bad year 75 per cent of children born would be dead within twelve months.

Nevertheless, this state of affairs was held to be all very proper: 'whatever is, is right.' Each man's place in society, however miserable that place might be, was fixed by divine order.

Order is Heaven's first law; and thus confessed
Some are, and must be, greater than the rest,
More rich, more wise, but who infers from hence
That such are happier, shocks all common sense.

–this is Pope again. Soame Jenyns went even further: 'the sufferings of individuals are absolutely necessary to universal happiness', he said, and the poor in any case had their 'opiate', ignorance, 'a cordial, administered by the gracious hand of providence'. What a shame it would be, he declared, to deprive them of this opiate by educating them.

We may be, and indeed should be, shocked by such opinions; but they were not untypical of eighteenth-century belief. And the order which such men as Pope and Jenyns claimed to have found within human society, they also thought applied to cosmic things. Man was a little lower than the angels, perhaps, but on a higher plane than the monkey and the mosquito.

The more perceptive minds of the time, of course, saw through this philosophy at once. The barb of satire was their weapon. Either they could, as Voltaire did, reduce these ideas to absurdity by writing with tongue in cheek, 'Everything is for the best in the best of all possible worlds', and 'If God did not exist, it would be necessary to invent him'; or they could tell stories, as Swift did in *Gulliver's Travels*, which on the surface seem innocent enough, yet contain such biting remarks as this, from the 'Voyage to Brobdingnag', 'I cannot but conclude the bulk of your natives to be the most pernicious race of little odious vermin that nature ever suffered to crawl upon the face of the earth.'

The bubble of smugness proved hard to prick. Most of those who read Swift and Voltaire at all were left unmoved. They did not even perceive the irony in Swift's *Modest Proposal* that the babies of over-populated Ireland would make very tasty eating, and from their skins could be fashioned 'Gloves for Ladies, and summer boots for Fine Gentlemen'. They actually thought he meant it. In any case, it was far more comfortable to go on believing that all things, including the structure of society, were ordained by God, and far more comfortable to maintain that the poor – as long as you were not one of them – performed a useful function in serving and supporting the well-to-do.

As far as the arts were concerned, it was generally agreed that the teeming masses could be ignored, and that the arts were for the benefit of a small, leisured and on the whole wealthy group. Whether fine or applied, liberal or mechanical, mattered little; the main thing was that they should be 'polite'. They were chiefly intended for the coffee-house élite, for those who passed their time agreeably if perhaps aimlessly sipping, talking, reading the papers and moving on only to sip, talk and read the papers elsewhere. Such an audience expected to be entertained, rather than stirred by what they read and saw; they expected, and on the whole they got, a certain objectivity on the artist's part. Whatever the medium, the manner was often more important than the content. In Pope's words, 'What oft was thought, but ne'er so well expressed' might be preferred to originality.

Seeking a model, the artists frequently found one in Greek and Roman classics. This happened in literature as well as the visual arts. The Latin-derived word was preferred to the Anglo-Saxon, poetry was shackled into alexandrines and heroic couplets.

During the first half of the eighteenth century, there developed among the English aristocracy the habit of the Grand Tour, perhaps just one summer, or even three or four years spent travelling on a cultural excursion through France, Italy and Germany. This was becoming a kind of peripatetic finishing-school for the proper education of young gentlemen. For some it may have been a complete waste of time and money, but the aims, according to Dean Tucker's *Instructions for Travellers*, were these: **First, to make curious Collections, as Natural Philosophers, Virtuosos, or Antiquarians. Secondly, to improve in Painting, Architecture and Music. Thirdly, to obtain the reputation of being Men of Vertu, and of an elegant Taste. Fourthly, to acquire foreign Airs, and adorn their dear Persons with fine Cloaths and new Fashions, and their Conversations with new Phrases. Or Fifthly, to rub off local Prejudices (which is indeed the most commendable Motive though not the most prevailing) and to acquire that impartial view of Men and Things, which no one single country can afford.**

Sometimes the Grand Tour had lasting influence and sparked off life-long enthusiasms. It left its mark on the design of buildings such as Mereworth in Kent, which is closely modelled on Palladio's Villa Rotonda in northern Italy. The tour was planned on a lavish scale. Thomas

Circular Hall, Mereworth Castle, Kent; designed by Colen
Campbell, 1723

Above 'Marriage à la Mode' II, painting by William
Hogarth, about 1743. The dissolute and disillusioned young
couple is seen among oppressively four-square furnishings—
the room is said to be based on Walpole's house at
5 Arlington Street. The mantelpiece ornaments caricature the
growing taste for Chinese porcelain.

Right Detail from 'An English Family at Tea', painting by
J van Aken. The decorous if abstracted family is using a
silver tea-kettle, probably English, and porcelain cups,
probably Chinese. The tea-caddy would normally be kept
locked.

Opposite page top The Mirror Drawingroom in the
Amalienburg, near Munich, designed by Cuvilliés, 1734–9

Opposite page below Chocolate-pot, jug and covered
dish, part of a service given by Louis XV to Marie Leczinska
in 1729. Silver by H N Cousinet

Coke of Norfolk, for instance, travelled in a coach and six with a retinue of servants, spending money like water–he was known as 'Il Cavaliere'. While abroad, he met Lord Burlington, the connoisseur, and the promising young designer, William Kent. Later (1734) he commissioned Kent to design not only the buildings of Holkham Hall, but also all the furnishings, so that it would be a fitting place in which to house the splendid collection of art treasures which he had brought back from Europe.

But, while in England classical sculptures were being settled into classical, Palladian-inspired, country houses, abroad there was a new movement afoot–the Rococo. An elegant, gay, playful style, it was derived from the arabesques beloved of Renaissance design, given a new freedom and rhythm. Natural forms, plants, flowers and shells, were very much a part of it (the word itself comes from the French *rocaille*, meaning pebble-work). These are not allowed to sprawl in confusion, but are caught up into the convention of the S-curve. The Rococo movement began in France (it is seen at its most entrancing in the paintings of Watteau, but he combined it with a tender mysticism all his own); it then moved to Germany where its supreme expression, architecturally, is the Mirror Drawingroom in the Amalienburg, Munich.

In England, the Rococo had little currency. One may say, perhaps, that William Hogarth's ideal of the serpentine line of beauty–on which, he claimed, the best artists' compositions were based–had something to do with it, but then Hogarth did not always put his theories into practice. There are some traces of rococo in Chippendale's 'Chinese' chairs, in plaster work, perhaps also in Chelsea porcelain, and one can find a literary parallel in Pope's exquisite confection of a poem, 'The Rape of the Lock'.

The Rococo was too frivolous a style to suit English taste, but in Germany and France it was found apt and delightful for most of the applied arts, as well as for architecture and painting. It lent itself to furniture, to silver, and above all to pottery and porcelain.

The Statue Gallery, Holkham Hall, Norfolk, designed by William Kent for Thomas Coke's collection of antique sculpture, 1734

French writing-table, attributed to Charles
Cressent (1689–1768). Deal with
mahogany veneer, bronze mounts and
black morocco-leather top

Salon Bleu Régence, at the Musée
Carnavalet, Paris, showing French rococo
furnishings

Porcelain was a major preoccupation of the eighteenth century. The vogue began as a cult of the exotic. People were fascinated by the fine wares imported from China. (In fact, the Chinese potters did not produce their very finest wares for export, but the Europeans were not to know that.) These were closely associated with the growing habit of tea-drinking. Tea never became the social drink that coffee did—one drank it with one's family or friends at home, with the exorbitantly expensive dried leaves themselves safely locked away from thieving servants.

One could do nothing about the price of tea, and there was no alternative to importing it. Porcelain, however, was another matter. At Meissen in Germany, scientific experiments ultimately produced a true hard-paste porcelain, what is popularly known as 'Dresden china'. Of course it was still mainly earthenware, delft, faïence and the rest, that was made and used throughout Europe, but porcelain so much embodies the spirit of eighteenth-century art that it is fair to say that with Meissen, the Age of Porcelain had begun.

Top French earthenware bowl in the shape of a cabbage: Strasbourg

Above Ewers and vase of Chinese celadon, mounted in France, 1745–9, with chased and gilt bronze

Left Bohemian 'Zwischengoldglas'. The gold design is enclosed between two layers of glass

German porcelain figure of Harlequin, made by J J Kändler of Meissen, about 1738

Furniture

By the early 1700s, the brilliance of the Sun King, Louis XIV, who had reigned in France with such splendour during the latter part of the seventeenth century, was beginning to fade somewhat. The wars with Britain, Holland and Austria, culminating in shattering defeats by Marlborough, proved so expensive that even Louis had to economise a little. All his silver furniture was melted down. The panoply of court life was no longer on a super-human scale; and the trend was towards smaller and more intimate rooms.

Less formal living led to a lighter style and greater variety of furniture. Innovations included corner cupboards, and writing-desks for ladies which the French call 'bonheurs-du-jour' (literally translated, 'pleasures of the day').

Louis XIV was succeeded by his great-grandson Louis XV, but while he was still young, the country was ruled by a regent, Philip, Duke of Orleans, Louis XIV's nephew. This period, which, historically, lasted from 1710 to 1723, but artistically, some twelve years longer, is known as the *Régence*. In furniture, it saw the beginnings of a new elegance and lightness of design. Boulle marquetry, which was still fashionable during the last years of Louis XIV, now gave way to wood marquetry. Trade with the West Indies (some of the islands were French) introduced a number of new woods, the most important of which was to be mahogany, but also there were decorative ones suitable for marquetry, such as satinwood, rosewood and purplewood.

Venetian state chair, one of a set of eight. Carved and gilt pinewood, upholstered in velvet brocade, first half of the 18th century

Lacquer was also fashionable and there were some not very successful attempts to make the panels in France. Mostly, however, they were imported from the Far East.

More comfortable and practical furniture was designed. Chairs became wider and deeper, lower in the seat. They were no longer intended to be ranged in formal rows against the walls, therefore they could be lighter in form. Rococo designs, such as those of Juste-Aurèle Meissonnier, were beginning to influence the prevailing style. The leading cabinet-maker of the day (he was also something of a sculptor) was Charles Cressent, 1685–1768. Cressent produced work of very fine quality and made much use of bronze mounts. He liked to make these himself, for which practice he was prosecuted by the guilds of bronze casters, chasers and gilders, who looked on this as their department.

The style of furniture known as Louis XV began about 1735 and ended in 1760. Rococo design was now given full play. Structural lines were often concealed by a plethora of S-curved bronze decoration. The emphasis was even more on comfort. Feminine taste prevailed: furniture was usually painted in light pastel colours and white, with touches of gold or silver. New items included the 'bureau à pente' (a ladies' writing

French armchair, walnut, about 1715–20

desk with a sloping lid), sofas of various kinds, day-beds (often in two or three separate parts) and 'commodes' (marble-topped chests either with three drawers, or with two small drawers set above two larger ones; the chests were made with 'bombé' or swelling fronts, usually designed as if they were one whole panel). The 'bureaux plats' were used by men; these were simply large tables with long legs, three drawers and a flat top.

In 1743 there was a general tightening up of guild regulations. Beside the guilds, there were free-lance craftsmen, mainly of German descent; their prices were generally lower. To distinguish the guilds' work, every piece had to be stamped with a 'maindron', an iron bar which bore the maker's name in relief. The only exception was furniture made specifically for the Crown, and this did not have to be stamped.

The labour of furniture-making was very precisely divided up. There was the joiner (*menuisier*), who worked the solid wood; the carver; the gilder and painter; then the cabinet-makers (*ébénistes*) who did the finer work and veneering; and finally the bronze workers—*fondeurs-ciseleurs* who cast and chased the bronze, and *ciseleurs-doreurs* who gilded it. One worked as an apprentice for a number of years and then, on approval of a test-piece, became a master-craftsman.

Such was the situation in France where, it was generally agreed, the most fashionable furniture was made. French rococo was a potent influence in countries as diverse as Italy, Spain and Russia. The Italians combined it with their preference for ornate styles in heavy-looking materials, such as marble, gesso and semi-precious stones (*pietra dura*). In Spain, the Italian-born designer Matias Gasparini chose the Louis XV style when decorating the royal appartments in Madrid. In

French wardrobe with clock, ornamented with 'Boulle' marquetry and bronze mounts, mid-18th century

Dutch bureau-bookcase veneered with burr-walnut, about 1740

Russia, Bartolommeo Rastrelli (a Russian, but of Italian descent) used an opulent version of rococo to adorn the Palace of Tsarskoe Zelo in St Petersburg.

Germany, too, followed the rococo style; Cuvilliés, who designed the Amalienburg outside Munich, had studied in Paris and thus set the pattern for the furniture-makers to follow – a bold and exuberant development of *Régence*. German cabinet-makers frequently used lacquer panels. They also developed a new type of furniture in the knee-hole desk.

In the Low Countries, as well, lacquer was popular. Because of their trade with the East, the Dutch enjoyed a virtual monopoly of Japan lacquer, and they made their own imitations, more successfully than the French. French design, particularly rococo, came to Holland through the Huguenot refugees, but English taste was also influential. The Dutch developed great skill in marquetry, with a preference for flower designs. Some cabinets and bureau-bookcases were made with cornices specially designed to provide standing-place for the prized Chinese porcelain.

In England, furniture had, in general, a classical solemnity. It was very much influenced by architecture. The *Four Books of Architecture* by the sixteenth-century Italian architect Palladio had been translated and published in English and this had renewed interest in the English seventeenth-century architect, Inigo Jones, whose work was much influenced by Palladio's.

Then Colen Campbell's *Vitruvius Britannicus*, the first volume published in 1715, had strengthened further the cause of classicism. It is hardly surprising, then, that in the first half of the eighteenth century, taste in furniture was swayed above all by a man who was architect as well as designer–William Kent. His furniture is heavy and sculptural, almost baroque in style.

In Queen Anne's reign, chairs were made with 'cabriole' legs and ball-and-claw feet. Furniture, already architectural in form, was generally veneered in walnut on an oak or pine carcase. New pieces included bureau-bookcases, and card tables with receptacles for money. After 1720, there was difficulty in obtaining walnut, and it was gradually superseded by mahogany.

Although some designs of lighter line, influenced by the French, were introduced by William Jones in 1739 in his *Gentlemen's or Builder's Companion*, it was not until the 1750s that the English used the rococo style with much confidence.

Ceramics

A Jesuit missionary, Père d'Entrecolles, stationed in China in the early eighteenth century, wrote in letters back to Paris detailed accounts of how the Chinese made porcelain. He told not only how the kaolin and the petuntse rock (the essential basic ingredients) were prepared, but also how the factories were organized on mass-production lines: one piece of porcelain might pass through the hands of as many as seventy

American marriage-chest in oak and other woods, Connecticut River Valley, 1710–15. The initials MB stand for Martha Bridgeman

Chinese cabinet on stand, early 18th century

workmen. As for the decoration, prototypes were made and then copied: **All the science of these painters,** Père d'Entrecolles writes, **and indeed of Chinese painters in general, is based on no principles and only consists of a certain routine helped by a limited turn of imagination ... The painting is distributed in the same workshop among a great number of workmen. One workman does nothing but draw the first colour line beneath the rims of the pieces; another traces flowers, which a third one paints; this man is painting water and mountains, and that one either birds or other animals. Human figures are generally treated the worst.**

D'Entrecolles described every technique used by the Chinese in the manufacture of porcelain, even how the kiln was packed and how much fuel was needed – 180 loads of pine, at 133 pounds weight each load, were burnt at every firing. He concludes: **It is not surprising that porcelain is so dear in Europe for ... it is rare for a furnace to succeed completely; often everything is lost, and on opening it the porcelain and the cases will be found converted into a solid mass as hard as rock. Moreover, the porcelain that is exported to Europe is almost always fashioned after new models, often of bizarre character, and difficult to reproduce; for the least fault they are refused, and remain in the hands of the potters, because they are not in the taste of the Chinese and cannot be sold to them.**

French faïence dish, decorated in blue on white in 'à la Berain' design, Moustiers, 1720–40

Obviously the Chinese did not find it altogether easy working for the European market, but the information which Père d'Entrecolles had at first hand was such that many European potters and their patrons would have given their right hands to possess it.

A German aristocrat with scientific leanings called Walter von Tschirnhaus was carrying out experiments with fusible clays. In Saxony he met Johann Friedrich Böttger, alchemist to the Elector Augustus I. Together they set about analysing and firing all the minerals of Saxony, the purpose being in Tschirnhaus's case to make synthetic silver, in Böttger's to make gold. Needless to say, in neither enterprise were they successful, but from their thorough-going experiments they discovered – for the first time in Europe – how to make hard-paste porcelain.

Tschirnhaus died in 1708. Meanwhile the Elector had been losing patience with Böttger (as an alchemist the man was a flop!) and kept him imprisoned in the Albrechtsburg fortress at Meissen. However, making the best of Böttger's discoveries, the Elector established there in 1710 the first European porcelain factory. Böttger was sworn to secrecy, but shortly before he died he revealed the recipe (he was drunk at the time) to Konrad Hunger, one of the Meissen workers. There followed a period when wandering arcanists (the term is derived from the Latin word for 'secret') travelled from court to court, claiming to know the skill of porcelain-making.

The earliest Meissen porcelain is decorated in enamels, brownish-red, rose-pink and turquoise – no cobalt blue until after 1725. At first the

Giant white Meissen porcelain peacock by J J Kändler, 1731–5

factory produced only small pieces, but as time progressed the Elector required larger and more ambitious pieces. He was also interested in developing porcelain sculpture, and for this employed a young man called Johann Joachim Kändler, who had trained as a sculptor. Kändler produced, with astonishing success, enormous animal figures for the Elector's Japanese Palace. He also made, as well as comparatively useful wares, very vigorous little Commedia dell'Arte figures of harlequins and the like.

In France, there had been experiments in porcelain manufacture from the late seventeenth century, but because there is no kaolin, or china-clay, in France, and because the Germans guarded their stocks of it as closely as they did their secrets, the French developed the manufacture of soft-paste porcelain. The materials used were frit–made of, for instance, sand, saltpetre, salt, chalk, soda and alum mixed, fired and ground up–then mixed with clay. Lacking homogeneity, soft paste was less strong, less versatile, but it was fired at a lower temperature, therefore a greater colour range was possible. Early factories were at Rouen, where they chiefly made earthenware, and St Cloud, but it was not until the second half of the eigh-

teenth century that France became the leading country for porcelain manufacture.

Most early porcelain factories operated at a loss. Their products were principally for court use, or for gifts. The general public could not afford it, nor perhaps did they like it. Their choice was earthenware. This too was new, in that now dinners all over Europe were usually eaten from earthenware plates and not from wooden or pewter platters. In France, the Rouen style influenced the other factories at Moustiers, Marseille and Strasbourg. At Moustiers they developed an elegant style of decoration based on designs by Jean Berain, while at Strasbourg they preferred naturalistic forms which they sometimes took to extremes.

Earthenware was also made in Germany (Hamburg, Potsdam and Frankfurt), very much on the lines that it was still made in Holland. Blue and white predominated. In England, a new range of colours was developed at Liverpool. Meanwhile the Staffordshire slipware tradition continued to produce useful wares of somewhat rural character.

Silver

In both France and England, silversmiths were patronized not only by the royalty and aristocracy, but by the middle classes. Their art was encouraged by the popularity of tea, coffee and chocolate drinking, but it was prosperity that made it possible. England, in particular, was developing as an aggressively mercantile and self-confident nation. Foreign visitors remarked on this. Here is de Saussure, a Swiss, in 1727: **I do not think there is a people more prejudiced in its own favour than the British people, and they allow this to show in their talk and manners. They look on foreigners in general with contempt, and think nothing is as well done elsewhere as in their own country.** But the art of the silversmith at the time depended very largely on the skill of Huguenot refugees.

At the very beginning of the eighteenth century there came a reaction to the elaborate and ebullient forms of baroque silver, and a preference for plainer forms. The hexagonal Powderham Dish made by Benjamin Pyne in 1698 represents a transitional phase, for although the dish is severely geometrical in form, the lines of the engraving are still flowing and voluptuous. The flagon made in London about 1702 by the Huguenot silversmith Pierre Platel shows some-

English Staffordshire slipware jug, with sgraffito decoration, possibly by Ralph Shaw, 1730–40

thing of the new trend towards plainness, yet the masks on either side are still richly baroque. For simple elegance we have to turn to Paris.

The French were in silver, as in many other arts, the leaders of European design, but few French pieces have survived in their country of origin, because there was another great melting-down during the Revolution at the end of the century. It is in France, around 1730, that we first find in silver that rococo style that was also

being pioneered in furniture and interior decorating. Pieces begin to be embellished with natural and asymmetrical forms and the S-curve which (in Hogarth's words) 'leads the eye a wanton sort of chase'. Despite its use of rococo ornament, French silver always maintains a certain reticence, and basic shapes are never altogether lost. This was not so in Germany, where even at the beginning of the century work in precious metals sometimes indulged in the wildest extravagances.

French Chocolate-pot, by H N Cousinet (see page 58)

German jasper bowl mounted in gold with jewels, enamels and cameos, illustrating the Labours of Hercules, by Melchior Dunglinger, 1712

Silver cake-basket by Paul de Lamerie, about 1730

English silver flagon, by Pierre Platel, about 1702

Glass

The story of glass in the first half of the century was very much influenced by political events. The Treaty of Utrecht in 1713 had permitted Central European glass-makers to sell their wares in western Europe. Then the accession of George, Elector of Hanover, to the throne of England in the following year further encouraged the dissemination of continental styles; and later, European glass-makers followed in his wake.

But in one respect, and that the most important, England retained her superiority in glass-making. The metal containing lead, which had been developed by Ravenscroft towards the end of the seventeenth century, was much better than anything produced elsewhere. There were now eleven glasshouses in London making lead glass, five in Stourbridge and four in Bristol. The glass they made had a new strength and clarity. It is,

however, softer in appearance than the hard brilliance of modern glass, and has a light-diffusing quality.

The third political measure to influence the design of glass in this period was the most drastic and the most direct. In 1745, the first Glass Excise Act was passed in Britain, imposing a tax of one penny a pound weight on flint glass— including any glass removed from the finished piece, so that discouraged both cutting and deep engraving. Glass consequently became lighter and thinner in section. The Act did not apply to Ireland, so glass design there was not affected; however, Irish glass was made for the home market only, as it was not allowed to be imported into England.

It is characteristic of this new trend towards lightness that one of the favourite decorative devices was the 'air-twist'. This developed from a single bubble of air, or 'tear' left in the glass.

English Jacobite glasses: air-twist stem wine-glasses with rose and thistle emblems, mid-18th century

It was found that by elongating and interweaving these 'tears', a brilliant decorative effect could be produced. Air-twists were mainly used to embellish the stems of wine-glasses; they had the practical advantage of being weightless.

Certain special glasses were made to symbolize the secret fervour of the Jacobite movement, promoted by some Scots but far more by prosperous English Catholic squires. Jacobite glasses were ornamented with roses and/or thistles, oakleaves and inscriptions (the symbolism becomes complex and obscure in its details), so that they could drink the toast of 'The King over the Water.' Most of them did it as a kind of game; few—as the Pretenders found to their cost—were serious supporters. The engraved glasses remain, however, and have a special fascination because of their associations.

German glass was not taxed in the same way that the British was, and so forms continue heavy. Some very skilful wheel-engraving was done, particularly at Potsdam where they achieved a remarkably three-dimensional effect with their characteristic deep cutting.

Bohemia was already famous for her coloured and gilded glass. Now she developed a new decorative technique—that of the 'Zwischengläser'. A design in gold leaf was enclosed between two layers of glass, thus rendering it permanent and not subject to abrasion as surface gilding is.

In actual manufacture, the Dutch could not compete with the English on the one side and the Germans and Bohemians on the other, but they did still excell at engraving. Generally they used English glass for this, lead glass being superior to lime glass for the purpose.

German beaker and cover with wheel engraving of bacchanalian scenes, by Gottfried Spiller of Potsdam, about 1700.

Dutch wine-glass engraved by Frans Greenwood, 1720, with figures from Jacques Callot's 'Balli di Sfessania'. Callot's etching of Scapino and Captain Zerbino is shown below.

Scapino.   Cap: Zerbino

1750–1800

'Private happinesss is the proper and ultimate end of all our actions whatever.' So Bishop Law had written, and probably most men in the second half of the eighteenth century would have agreed with him. A few, the social reformers, would have been worried by that word 'private', but on the whole it was considered reasonable that the well-being of the few should depend on the subservience of the many. This was the accepted order of society.

The main problem was this: was happiness more likely to be found through man-made things, or was it to be sought through a harmony with the natural world? The second half of the eighteenth century saw in general a progression from the former to the latter way of thinking.

To begin with, most men of culture liked to keep Nature strictly under control, and many preferred an urban way of living anyway. Dr Johnson was one of these. 'When a man is tired of London he is tired of life', he asserted, and viewed with a certain disdain wilder prospects than London could afford. Even Gray, whom one thinks of as something of a nature poet and associates with country churchyards, was so appalled by rugged landscapes that when his coach was passing through the Cumberland hills he drew down the blinds. Although many rich men, especially in England, were devoted to their country estates and some, like Coke of Norfolk, led the field in agrarian reform, most still looked on nature as something to be checked, controlled and subjugated: she must not have her own unbridled way. Typical of mid-eighteenth century opinion was Lancelot 'Capability' Brown, the landscape-gardener, whose characteristic remark (and the one which gave him his nickname) on being called to survey an estate was 'I see great capability of improvement here'.

Everything had to be tidied up, neatened, straightened out, rules had to be obeyed, precedents had to be found; this was all part of good taste and the search for elegant perfection. Even spelling, previously idiosyncratic, was given a new importance; Lord Chesterfield wrote to his son in 1750, 'I must tell you that orthography, in the true sense of the word, is so absolutely necessary for a man of letters, or a gentleman, that one false spelling may fit a ridicule on him for the rest of his life. And I know a man of quality who never recovered the ridicule of having spelled *wholesome* without the "W"'. In the pursuit of elegance the aristocracy spared no expense, especially in France, where court life was at its most lavish and luxurious. 'Après nous le déluge', declared Madame de Pompadour: the great flood will come after our time. Meanwhile it was a time to eat, drink and be merry—but not, of course, in any vulgar way, for the French set the tone for the rest of Europe.

The English way of life was more down-to-earth or, as one might say, pedestrian. A love of sociability, rather than the solitariness which came later, led to the formation of clubs. These had developed from the coffee-houses of earlier in the century. To be what Dr Johnson called a 'clubbable' man was high praise indeed. 'Let me smile with the wise', said the Doctor, 'and feed with the rich' Johnson was a realist, always forceful in his opinions, justified or not, and thunderingly plain-spoken. A dogmatic and sometimes a difficult man, he dominated intellectual society; to his club flocked Sir Joshua Reynolds, Oliver Goldsmith, David Garrick and even Edmund Burke, all distinguished men in very different walks of life, and they counted themselves honoured by his company. And as for Boswell, his biographer, he was more than honoured, he was overwhelmed.

To aid the search for perfection, which was an English preoccupation as well as a French, men looked to see what might be culled from other civilizations. 'He who resolves never to ransack any mind but his own', said Reynolds in his Academy address of 1770, 'will soon be reduced, from mere barrenness, to the poorest of all imitations; he will be obliged to imitate himself.' The strongest influence of all was that of classical antiquity, chiefly Roman. The Grand Tour, which was growing ever more popular, was rarely extended beyond Italy on the one hand and the Pyrenees on the other; Spain was considered too barbarous and uncomfortable, and Greece likewise, for it was under Turkish domination. Greek art was admired, as

Claydon House, Buckinghamshire: the recess in the
Chinese Room, about 1765.

far as it was known. The German critic, Johann Winckelmann, whose writings did much to
found the neo-classical style, wrote in 1755, 'Good taste, which is spreading more and more
throughout the world, had its beginning under a Greek sky'. But it was generally believed
that the best of Greek art could be seen without going further than Italy.

Interest in Roman art had been given added impetus by the discoveries in 1748 of the
ancient cities of Herculaneum and Pompeii. Their influence was immediate and widespread.
It was particularly strong in designers such as Robert Adam, who brought to their interiors
and indeed to almost all the applied arts, a new gaiety and lightness, still within the classical
idiom. This style, which was commonly known as 'Etruscan', was used by Adam at Osterley
Park for instance and, also by Wedgwood, who called his pottery Etruria. In the field of
literature, too, Rome was very much in favour. Edward Gibbon (1737–1794) wrote his
'Decline and Fall of the Roman Empire', and he recounted the source of inspiration thus:
'It was at Rome, on the 15th of October, 1764, as I sat musing amidst the ruins of the Capitol,
while the barefoot friars were singing vespers in the Temple of Jupiter, that the idea of writing
the decline and fall of that city first started to my mind.'

There was another sort of classicism too: that of the Italian Renaissance. Reynolds
coming to Rome as a young man was rather impressed by Raphael, but absolutely bowled
over by Michelangelo. When Reynolds later became the first president of the Royal Academy
(founded 1768), it was above all Michelangelo's works that he urged his students to study.

Left door **right** fireplace. Details from the Chinese Room, Claydon House. The woodcarving is by Lightfoot, a local craftsman, about 1765.

Lest too much classicism should become tedious, however, the English in particular enjoyed a few eccentric variations. Just as they felt their estates might be improved by the addition of a few mock ruins, or a grotto, or even an artificial hermit (employed at a regular salary provided that he kept himself in a sufficiently unhygienic state), so they often liked the insides of their houses to have a touch of the 'Gothick'. This was mock-medieval: the final 'k' distinguishes it from the real thing. And what could be done with a decorative interior could also be done with a chair; designers were required to be versatile.

China, and the European idea of China – which it is convenient to call *chinoiserie* – remained a potent influence. Not many architects and designers went to China as Sir William Chambers did, to study the arts there at first hand. Chambers admired the Chinese work principally for this reason: 'Whatever is really Chinese has at least the merit of being original; these people seldom or never copy or imitate the inventions of other nations.' He popularised *chinoiserie* by publishing, in French and English, *Designs for Chinese Buildings, Furniture, Dresses, Machines, and Utensils.*

Elegance permitted such variations. But in France it was a fool's paradise the aristocracy enjoyed, too precious to last. The old régime had been too unbending, too autocratic, too inbred, and now the crash came. Its reverberations were felt all over Europe. Edmund Burke wrote in his *Reflections on the Revolution in France*: **It is now sixteen or seventeen years since I saw the Queen of France, then the Dauphiness, at Versailles; and surely never lighted on this orb, which she hardly seemed to touch, a more delightful vision ... glittering like the morning star, full of life and splendour and joy ... Little did I dream that I should have lived to see disasters fallen upon her in a nation of gallant men, in a nation of men of honour, and of cavaliers ... The age of chivalry is gone. That of sophisters, economists and calculators has succeeded; and the glory of Europe is extinguished for ever.'**

Certain it was that in France a whole generation of patrons had gone to the guillotine. The artists and craftsmen were left for the most part with no-one to work for. This applied particularly to the applied arts; the painters did better. Some, like Jacques-Louis David, found inspiration in the situation.

For not everyone took Burke's gloomy view. There were some on his side of the Channel who watched developments in France with bated breath; was it possible that government by the people would work, that a nation could actually be ruled by principles of liberty, fraternity and equality? In any case, some Englishmen were disillusioned with their own governments (the poet Wordsworth was one of them). But finding that events in France could not, after all, be recorded to their own idealism, some of them advocated anarchy.

In order, however, to be able to attach themselves to some ideal, they tended to make a god out of Nature. A love of Nature was not new; the German poet Goethe, writing in the early 1770s, imagined that he had collected in his handkerchief scraps of grass, moss, leaves, flowers and small creatures during a country walk, and how European fashion would scorn these natural things. ' "It is in trivial taste" says the Italian, and passes by. "Childishness", stammers the Frenchman and triumphantly snaps his snuff-box à la Grecque.' Goethe goes on to attack the Latin races for their slavish imitation of the classical, for measuring rather than feeling.

'How idle it would be', said William Godwin, 'to wish to change our arbours, our verdant lanes and thickets, for vaulted roofs, and gloomy halls, and massy plate!' In Nature, the philosophers felt, there was a general and celestial pattern, a harmony to which man should endeavour to attune himself. This required solitariness, or at least a meeting of no more than two or three congenial spirits; it was not the attitude of the 'clubbable' man. It was a way of thinking which affected the literary arts profoundly. On the visual arts, however, it had less impact. The classical remained the prevailing style. As far as the applied arts were concerned, lines became even straighter, finer, simpler; the ideal was a cold perfection.

English Romantic Revival interior: The Strawberry Room from Lee Priory, Littlebourne, near Canterbury. Designed by James Wyatt, 1782–92

French neoclassical interior: Marie Antoinette's boudoir at Versailles, about 1780

Furniture

The discovery in 1748 of the ancient Roman
cities of Herculaneum and Pompeii led to the
emergence of the neo-classical style. This happened astonishingly quickly, largely because the
brother of Madame de Pompadour, the French
King's mistress (who was obviously in a position
to influence court taste if he wanted to) was the
very next year touring Italy.

It received little encouragement at first from
the King himself, but he allowed Madame de
Pompadour and Madame du Barry to indulge
their whims, and they were its chief promoters.
At first, the neo-classical existed alongside the
rococo style associated with the reign of Louis
XV, and this period of furniture design between
1760 and 1770 is known as the *Transitional*.
Finally Neo-Classical won the day, and rococo
furniture was produced only by provincial
cabinet-makers. As early as 1763, Baron Grimm,
an artistic go-between, was observing 'Everything in Paris is *à la Grecque*'. Of course, it was not
really Greek at all, but Roman-inspired, as that
distinction was not yet understood.

The new trend was to replace rococo curves
with straighter lines and more rectilinear shapes.
The main exponent of the French Transitional
style was Jean-François Oeben. He was born in
Germany about 1720, trained in the workshop
of one of the sons of A C Boulle, and owed his
advancement to the patronage of Madame de
Pompadour. He was not made *maître* until 1760,
and died only three years later. Oeben was an
exceptionally fine marquetry designer, and also
liked to incorporate in his pieces secret drawers
and cunning mechanical devices.

Oeben having died youngish, his senior assist-
ant Riesener kept up the family business by
marrying his widow. Riesener was also a German, born near Essen in 1734, was made *maître*
in 1768, and lived long enough to enjoy the
patronage of Queen Marie Antoinette and to
endure the lack of patronage from the French
Revolution until his death in 1806.

Perhaps the most famous piece of furniture
ever made, and certainly the most splendid from
the Transitional period, King Louis XV's
writing-desk, was designed by these two men:
Oeben began it, Riesener completed it. It is a
roll-top desk, far more rococo than neo-classical.
The roll-top mechanism works at the turn of a
key, and the desk is ornamented with lavishly
ornate gilt mounts by the royal founder and
gilder Duplessis, and exquisite marquetry, probably by Riesener.

French armchair, pinewood carved and gilt, period of Louis
XVI

French pedestal-cabinet, oak veneered with ebony and
Boulle marquetry, bronze mounts and medallion of nymph
playing pipes to dancing satyr, late 18th century

Riesener's own style, however, was not fully developed until the opulent and extravagant time of Louis XVI. Sèvres porcelain had been developed, and Riesener found that plaques of this material incorporated in his pieces gave them a light and colourful effect. Rich marquetry was still popular as a finish, until about 1780, when there was a slight trend towards economy and it was found that mahogany with brass mounts (sometimes 'curl' figured veneers were used, cut from where the branches of a tree join the trunk) would produce almost as decorative an effect at far less coat. The legs of the flat-topped table-like writing desks became straight and tapering, chairs also became more rigid in line; at the same time there was a growing desire for comfort and an emphasis on fabrics.

During the *Directoire* period, the last decade of the century, the tendency was towards even straighter lines, less expensive materials, and an avoidance of exotic woods apart from mahogany. Deep and comfortable arm-chairs were no longer made. Their place was taken by day-beds with curved-over ends ('méridiennes' – the word means mid-day). The prevailing style was that brand of cool classicism known as 'Etruscan', and the most famous cabinet-maker associated with it was Georges Jacob.

Italy, Germany, Russia, Holland and Portugal followed the Parisian lead. It must be remembered how many of the first rank of French cabinet-makers were German in origin. Abraham Roentgen's son David worked both in France and Germany. His furniture shows the beginning of the neo-classical style in Germany, where the fashion for an exuberant rococo had lingered until about 1770.

In Russia, French cabinet-makers were brought to St Petersburg by Catherine the Great, and French styles were followed very closely there. She also received gifts of furniture from the French royal family, so that the furniture used at court can hardly be said to be Russian at all. At Tula, in Central Russia, an indigenous type of furniture was made of steel.

Apart from France, the most influential country for furniture-making was England. The second half of the eighteenth century was the greatest period for English furniture, and with it are associated four famous names: Chippendale, Adam, Hepplewhite and Sheraton. The emphasis in English furniture making had always tended to be on the qualities of the wood itself, and it was this tradition that was now continued and more finely developed.

Design for a mirror by Thomas Sheraton

French serinette, about 1770. Its purpose was to encourage cage-birds to sing

English commode with flower marquetry panel within lozenge design, about 1760

Thomas Chippendale (1718–1779), a Yorkshireman, set up his business in St Martin's Lane, London, in 1753, and in the following year produced his book of furniture designs *The Gentleman and Cabinet-Maker's Director*. **Gentlemen and Ladies,** ran the advertisement, **have now an Opportunity to gratify their taste with respect to Furniture, the designs being both various and elegant.** Immensely successful, the book established a Chippendale style, so that it is often hard to judge which pieces were by the master himself, and which (these are far more numerous) were done by other cabinet-makers from the designs in the *Director*. The Chippendale style spread not only throughout Britain but also in America, where a thriving school was established in Philadelphia. By the 1750s, the rococo style was being used in England with a certain amount of confidence. Chippendale adopted it, but he also introduced 'Gothick' and 'Chinese' variations. The wood he used was usually a fine quality mahogany. Some of the best furniture we know by Chippendale is that which he designed specifically for Harewood House.

Late Chippendale furniture is influenced by the style of Robert Adam (1728–1792), a Scotsman. Robert Adam and his three brothers had studied architecture under their father, and it

Two chair designs by George Hepplewhite from 'The Cabinet-Maker's and Upholsterer's Guide'

is as an architect, decorator and above all designer that we remember him. He was a furniture-designer, not a cabinet-maker. Having travelled in Italy shortly after the excavations of Pompeii and Herculaneum, he introduced the neo-classical style into Britain. He and his brother James, he claimed, 'have not trod in the paths of others' but 'brought about, in this country, a kind of revolution in the whole system of this useful and elegant art.' Adam furniture and Adam-inspired furniture feature (usually as an inlaid design) the palm-leaf and shell motifs, the urns, cameo-like panels and strings of flowers which derive from ancient Roman art.

Adam influenced profoundly the work of George Hepplewhite. Hepplewhite's origins are obscure. He is said to have come from Lancashire and he was actively in business in London from about 1775 until his death in 1786. His book of furniture designs called *The Cabinet-Maker's and Upholsterer's Guide* was published two years afterwards. Hepplewhite designed a variety of furniture, much of it inlaid, 'rational, simple, and withal, extremely elegant and refined'; but he is chiefly remembered for his shield-back chairs.

Towards the end of the century comes Thomas Sheraton (1751–1806), from Stockton-on-Tees. Although a cabinet-maker in his early years, by the time he established himself in Wardour Street, London, he was essentially a designer.

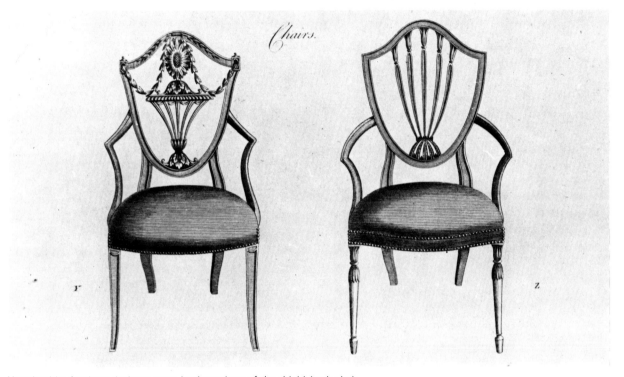

Hepplewhite furniture designs: open-back versions of the shield-back chair

Design by Sheraton from the 'Cabinet-Maker's and Upholsterer's Drawing Book', for 'A Summer bed in two compartments'

His trade card said that he 'teaches perspective, architecture and ornaments, makes designs for cabinet-makers, sells all kinds of drawing books.' He does not seem to have prospered in these enterprises, nor does he appear to have established a workshop. His importance in the history of furniture rests on his publications, in particular his *Cabinet-Maker's and Upholsterer's Drawing Book* which came out in four parts between 1791 and 1794. Sheraton designs are remarkable for their lightness and delicacy of treatment. They tend towards the straight and rectilinear rather than the curved. Some are delightful rather than practical and are unlikely ever to have been made. Sheraton died poor, obscure and insane. No piece of furniture can be definitely assigned to him.

Above English mahogany chair, mid-18th century, in the Chinese manner, possibly based on one of the designs shown below

Left Design by Robert Adam for an organ-case for the Duke of Cumberland, late 18th century

Below Designs for chairs in the Chinese manner, from Chippendale's 'The Gentleman and Cabinet-Maker's Director', 1754

American bonnet-top highboy in cherry-wood, Connecticut, 1760

American 'Brother's' slat-backed rocking-chair, of Shaker craftsmanship. Late 18th century

Ceramics

Nowhere in Europe in the second half of the eighteenth century was there anything to touch French porcelain. Bearing an affinity with Louis XV furniture and with the paintings of Watteau, Boucher and Fragonard, it epitomized the delicacy, the precision and the suavity of French culture.

It began as a triumph of ingenuity in overcoming a lack of natural resources of kaolin (china clay). The soft-paste porcelain developed in France was made from a great number of ingredients including the principal constituents of glass; it was a tricky process, and much ware was spoilt during manufacture, but because of the lower firing temperature, a greater colour range was possible. This possibly was fully explored in Sèvres porcelain.

The porcelain we call Sèvres started at Vincennes. In 1740, the brothers Gilles and Robert Dubois, who came from Chantilly, obtained permission to start a porcelain factory in some buildings of the Château de Vincennes near Paris. Their experiments seem to have continued only until 1744, then the secret appears to have been passed on to François Cravant. He, with Charles Adam, obtained a monopoly for Vincennes porcelain. It was forbidden for 'any persons, under pain of a fine of 3000 francs, unless it be those who have obtained letters-patent . . . either to set up or cause to be set up, any establishment for the production of porcelain.' A company was established and the King kept one third of the shares for himself. Thus royally protected, the factory received the name of 'Manufacture Royale des Porcelaines de France' and adopted its famous mark of two entwined Ls like the royal cipher. In 1756, possibly at the suggestion of Madame de Pompadour (whose name is very much associated with French porcelain), the factory was moved to the village of Sèvres. From 1760, the King became its sole owner. Although kaolin was discovered in 1768 near St Yrieix-la-Perche, and therefore hard-paste porcelain became feasible, it was little made until the 1780s, and even then soft-paste continued to be made as well.

Rococo design found full and free expression in French porcelain, even in the early wares made at Vincennes. Designs were based on natural forms of flowers, twigs, leaves and even butterflies. These first pieces were small-scale, but elegant and assured. A letter dated 21 September 1751, from Hultz, who was in charge

English porcelain: Chelsea figure group 'The Music Lesson' by J E Nilson, based on Boucher's painting 'L'Agréable Leçon'

The Porcelain Room for the royal villa at Portici, Capodimonte, near Naples, 1757–9

French porcelain: Sèvres ewer and basin in 'rose Pompadour' and gold, 1757

of the painting of the porcelain, states the aims which were so admirably achieved at Sèvres and Vincennes: 'let us shun what is heavy and trivial, and produce things that are light, delicate, new and varied . . .' Sèvres porcelain is famed for its use of colour: royal blue, turquoise, grass-green, yellow, carmine, tortoiseshell-brown, and the rich pink which in compliment to Madame, was named 'rose Pompadour'. Gold was employed particularly for surrounding 'reserve' decorative panels, and for all-over patterning, such as the tiny dotted circles known as *œil de perdrix* (partridge-eye).

Not all Sèvres and Vincennes wares are coloured, however. There are small statuettes which were left in the 'biscuit' (unglazed) state. They were based on designs by some of the most famous artists of the day. After about 1760, there was a tendency for the grace which had characterized the earlier wares to give way to mere splendour. The King sold Sèvres porcelain himself in his palace at Versailles, and the courtiers felt obliged to buy. Some full-scale dinner services were made. With the advent of hard-paste porcelain came a change of style to the prevailing neo-classical. After the downfall of the monarchy, the factory was taken over by the state, and the workers had a hard time of it

French porcelain: Sèvres biscuit figure of Cupid, after a model by Etienne-Maurice Falconet, 1758

until a more generous patronage was restored under Napoleon.

Other French porcelain factories of the late eighteenth century were at Rue du Petit Carrousel, Paris, at Deruelle in Clignancourt on the outskirts of Paris, and at Orleans, but all are of minor importance compared with Sèvres.

Porcelain was also made in Italy, notably at Capodimonte above Naples, where a factory was founded by Charles VII, King of the Two Sicilies, in 1743. No kaolin was available locally, therefore the porcelain was of the soft-paste variety. One of the most astonishing achievements in Capodimonte porcelain is a whole room in the palace of Portici panelled with porcelain slabs, decorated in relief with oriental figures, birds and flowers and branches. The chandelier and candlesticks are also of porcelain.

Another Italian factory, the Cozzi factory in Venice, specialized in producing coffee-jugs and cups for the Venetian nobility. They also provided the government, free of charge, with porcelain dishes for state occasions, and in return were granted certain privileges.

Detail from the Portici Porcelain Room (see p. 82): chinoiserie decoration in polychrome and gilt porcelain

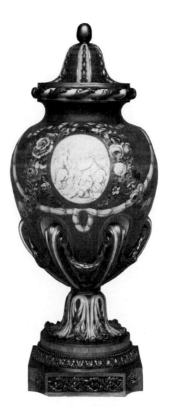

Above left Italian porcelain coffee-pot from the Cozzi Factory, Venice, about 1770

Above right Nymphenburg porcelain: Commedia dell'Arte figure of Julia, by F A Bustelli, about 1760

Right French porcelain: Sèvres vase and cover, blue with gold design, garlands of flowers and grisaille medallions, about 1769

Top Chinese painting of the inside of a dealer's shop, showing export porcelain, pictures and lacquered furniture

Above English rococo mirror, second half of the 18th century

French musical clock, bronze chased and gilt in the manner of J C Duplessis père (died 1774)

English Chinese-style bed, about 1750, probably by Thomas
Chippendale

British porcelain factories, unlike the continental ones, were commercial and independent enterprises. There was no royal or princely patronage. There were some short-lived experiments with hard-paste at Plymouth, Bristol and New Hall, but soft-paste porcelain was the general rule. The earliest of the English porcelain potteries was Chelsea, which was founded by a silversmith, Nicholas Sprimont, and started production in about 1743, apparently using a clay imported from the Cherokees in America. Then kaolin from Cornwall was used, obviously a cheaper alternative. It was mixed with ground glass (to give it translucency), sometimes bone-ash, and at Bristol they experimented with soap-rock. British porcelain design was generally

English black stoneware 'Etruscan' vase, decorated in imitation of Greek vase painting, Wedgwood, about 1770

Nymphenburg porcelain group, about 1760

derivative and owed much to Sèvres, Meissen and, of course, to oriental inspiration, but the statuette figures made by the Chelsea factory, and also perhaps the Bow and Derby factories, have considerable originality as well as charm, and are the finest achievement of British porcelain.

Even livelier figures were being made at the Nymphenburg factory in Bavaria by Franz-Anton Bustelli, who was engaged as a modeller by the Elector Maximilian Joseph in 1754. His delightful statuettes, many of them based on Commedia dell'Arte (Italian harlequinade) characters, are full of wit and elegance. Indeed, Nymphenburg porcelain figures may be said to embody the very spirit of rococo art.

The wares of Josiah Wedgwood in England were a case apart. They were at the time almost

Wedgwood jasper-ware vase, the decoration modelled in white on dark blue designed by John Flaxman and representing 'The Apotheosis of Homer', about 1786

the only fashionable ceramics not made of porcelain. Wedgwood did not always design for the luxury market, and his Queen's Ware (which was earthenware) set a new standard in practical, every-day pottery. This was perhaps his finest achievement, but he is chiefly remembered for his 'jasper' ware, which is a very fine stoneware incorporating a certain quantity of barium sulphate. Its natural colour would be white, but it was stained with oxides. Then it was decorated by the application of white reliefs inspired by antique cameos. Artists were commissioned to decorate jasper ware, and also the black stoneware vases which were painted in red and white in imitation of ancient Greek vases. The artists were not, of course, involved in the actual form of the pottery. Wedgwood wares are a clear evocation of the neo-classical ideal: they have purity and severity, cleanly cut lines, but at the same time, they are somewhat lifeless.

Silver

Designs in precious metals are perhaps a little slower to change than designs in other media, and the rococo style which one associates with the earlier decades of the eighteenth century did not reach its finest achievements in silver until the 1750s.

The comparatively few pieces of French silver to survive are nevertheless enough to indicate the quality of the workmanship. There is no doubt that some splendid things must have perished. One that has fortunately come down to us is the superb coffee-pot made in 1756 by François-Thomas Germain as part of a service for Joseph I of Portugal. The beauty of its swirling lines is all the greater because they are not without a certain restraint. The design is not allowed to run riot in the way that German rococo often did.

Within a decade tastes had changed, and a more sober, classical style prevailed. Many goldsmiths, in fact, had never practised the rococo style at all, and numerous plain pieces date from the same period as the most ornate. By 1770, 'massy plate' was being produced to grace royal dinner-tables, such as the soup-tureen made by Jacques Roettiers in Paris to the order of Catherine the Great of Russia–impressive, but heavy. Gradually the lines were fined down, but there is no dramatic change in style until after the Revolution.

Italian silver of the later eighteenth century

Early 18th-century tea-pot, stand and caddy (the rest of the silver is later) from 'A Family Taking Tea' (artist unknown)

Above 18th-Century shell ornament

Opposite page English delftware: Liverpool dish in 'Fazackerley' colours, about 1750

has a ponderous classicism, never as delicate and
sharp as the French – logical and restrained
rather than dramatic.

The English goldsmiths favoured very plain
designs indeed towards the end of the century.
The age of the Huguenot craftsmen was over,
and the work produced relied almost entirely on
the austere beauty of geometrical shapes. There
was very little ornamentation – an engraved
armorial shield, perhaps, and a beaded moulding
round the edge to emphasize the forms, nothing
more. Towards 1800, silver, influenced by the
designs of Robert Adam (which George III had
pronounced were 'too neat and pretty'), became
even more severe and elegant in form. Boat-
shapes and urn-shapes were commonly used,
square bases were in vogue, jugs were tall and
slender. There was little ornamentation except
a touch of discreet reeding or beading, or perhaps a band of bright-cut engraving. (Bright-
cutting was an English speciality and was made
by means of a V-shaped incision which reflects
light from one of the two facets.) It was a very
formal style; and it was as much in vogue in the
United States as it was in England.

French silver coffee-pot by François-Thomas Germain, part
of a service made for Joseph I of Portugal, 1756

American silver tea-service by Paul Revere of Boston, 1779.

Above Italian silver-gilt candlesticks, made in Turin, about 1780

Above French silver soup tureen by Jacques Roettiers Paris, 1770

Below English gold tea-pot and stand, by Daniel Smith and Robert Sharp, London, 1785

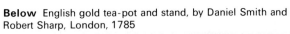

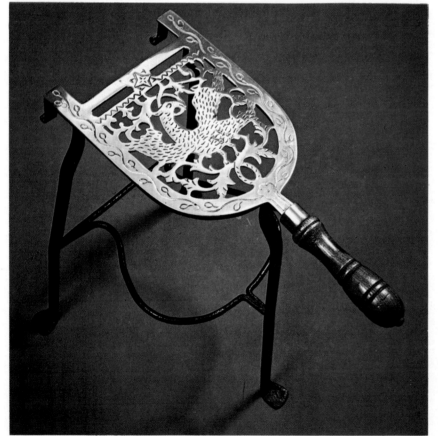

Above French Louis XVI period 'meuble d'appui', by J Dubois

Left American brass trivet (kettle-stand) about 1780

Opposite page top The Etruscan Room, Osterley Park: a neoclassical interior designed by Robert Adam, about 1775

Opposite page below Dining-sideboard designed by Robert Adam for Osterley Park, about 1775

Glass

By the middle of the eighteenth century the English were producing glass of unrivalled clarity. From about 1760, some of it has a hard brilliance due to the use of dioxide instead of protoxide of lead in its manufacture. Soda glass was still made, however, mainly in the north,

Dutch engraved glass by David Wolff, about 1780

and coloured glass was being developed, particularly in the Bristol area.

The clarity of the body or 'metal' of the best of English glass lent itself ideally to decoration. This took various forms. The fashion for air-twists continued until about 1770, but now there also developed the enamel-twist, in which threads of opaque white glass were used in a similarly decorative way. This was done between 1755 and 1780. For a decade, when both techniques were practised, they were sometimes used together on the same wine-glass.

Meanwhile the bowl of the glass, and also the bodies of larger pieces such as decanters, might be decorated in enamels. The English had not shown much skill in this art until William and Mary Beilby of Newcastle-upon-Tyne produced their first enamelling in the 1760s. Enamelling on glass is not the simple technique it might seem to be, for after painting, the glass must be fired, which requires precise temperature control, and it is also important that the metal and the enamel should contract at roughly the same rate. The early Beilby glasses (probably by William, who was older than his sister) are decorated with heraldic designs. Later the subjects included hops, barley, vines, birds, butterflies and even landscapes. The more ambitious glasses are done in colour as well as white monochrome.

Cut-glass was produced in England from 1760, but was not fully developed for another ten years, when 'crystal-cutting' was evolved, using diagonal cross cuts. With the fine quality of the metal, a brilliant effect was produced. Then the tax on glass was doubled, but at much the same time free trade was granted to Ireland. Consequently, English glass-makers, mainly from Bristol and Stourbridge, were shrewd enough to take their businesses abroad and establish glasshouses at Waterford, Cork and Belfast. A notice in the 'Dublin Evening Post' for 4 October 1783 said this: **Waterford Glass House. George and William Penrose have established an extensive glass manufacture in this city; their friends and the public may be supplied with all kinds of plain and flint glass, useful and ornamental.** The Waterford glass-works was probably the most important of the three, but the tendency has been to ascribe *all* Irish glass to Waterford, because the name was felt to have a certain cachet. The great period of Irish glass-making (which at least at the beginning was really English glass-making in Ireland) was a long one: 1780 to 1850.

It set a fashion on the continent. Where previously glass-works had tried to imitate Bohemian glass, now the 'façon d'Angleterre' (the English type of cut glass) was all the rage. It was made for instance, at the 'Manufacture des Cristaux et des Emaux de la Reine' at St Cloud, which started in 1783 and enjoyed the patronage of Marie-Antoinette.

In Holland, the ever-resourceful Dutch specialized in the art of engraving; although some glass was made in the country, they preferred to import English glass to work on. The technique of diamond stippled engraving introduced by Frans Greenwood was continued, notably by David Wolff.

Despite the departure of some workers to Ireland, Bristol retained her importance as a centre of glass-making, excelling in the making of coloured and opaque white glass. The Bristol works was especially famous for its dark blue glass, although colourless cut crystal was also made. The opaque white and the blue glass was frequently enamelled, the most famous of the artists in this field being Michael Edkins who was working at the Redcliffe (Buckinghamshire) glasshouse between 1762 and 1787. Glass which was a mixture of clear and opaque metals was also made both at Bristol and at Nailsea.

Glassware was slow to adopt the neo-classical styles popular in most of the other arts, and it was not until the very end of the century that there was an appreciable change in taste. One of the first indications was at Sèvres, where the technique of fusing biscuit-porcelain medallions into glass was evolved. These 'encrusted cameos' presage the cult of the antique which—in glass— would not have full sway until after the century had turned.

English glass: Bristol or Nailsea blue and white flask, late 18th century

Below Four Irish glass decanters, Waterford, 18th century

1800–1840

'It's only a step', said Napoleon with supreme callousness during the Retreat from Moscow, 'from the sublime to the ridiculous'. Napoleon Bonaparte, a Corsican soldier, had risen from rank to rank, had been appointed dictator ('First Consul') and finally Emperor. He was a man of ruthless ambition, shrewd but imaginative, and he drove himself hard; yet he had some personal magnetism which made men follow him even in his most foolhardy and fanatical attempts. One has to begin with Napoleon because this little man dominates the first part of the century. Revered in France, feared and detested in England as if he were some sort of ogre, he and his campaigns touched the lives of ordinary people all over Europe. At the height of his power, nearly the whole continent was included in his empire.

As for the British, the wars themselves may have impinged little on them, but the effects of wars were another matter. It was not only that a handful of poets and philosophers had looked to France to show them the way to a people's democracy, and that Napoleon's assumption of dictatorship had left them bitterly disappointed. Napoleon was defeated, to the relief and jubilation of his opponents, but there was a bill to pay. There had been a general rise in the cost of living. The Corn Laws which were passed in Britain from 1815 onwards helped agriculture, but only at the expense of the consumer. The Poor-Rate which weekly supplemented the income of 'poor and industrious persons' proved a very mixed blessing even to those who received it. People had ignored the warnings of Malthus ('Population, when unchecked,

Bedroom of the Empress Josephine at Malmaison, about 1810. Josephine had bought Malmaison during Napoleon's Egyptian campaign: this tent-like interior, although luxurious, is reminiscent of a military camp. The decorations are by Percier and Fontaine, the bed by Desmalter

increases in a geometrical ratio. Subsistence only increases in an arithmetical ratio') and there were more mouths to feed.

Industrialization was limited as yet and confined in the main to the new urban areas; but already it had brought about a decline in country craftsmanship. Villages were no longer self-contained, self-sufficient communities. There was a general improvement in communications – better roads, new railways, and the pace of life was faster. The life of the eighteenth-century cottager had not been all beer and skittles, but there was an ugliness about now which had not existed formerly. A man like William Cobbett, who took his 'Rural Rides' in the south and west of England, noticed and deplored it; 'I never liked to see machines,' he said, 'lest I should be tempted to endeavour to understand them'. The poet Robert Southey saw superficiality in the new type of civilization: 'the middle classes are veneered instead of being hearts of oak'.

At least there was one great step forward: a wider literacy. More people had the benefit of a smattering of education. Consequently the artists were working for a wider public. They became involved with politics and current events in a way they had not been previously. Goya's 'Disasters of War' etchings, for instance, dating from 1810–1813, show with unflinching realism the effects of war on ordinary people and common soldiery.

Society, then, felt the impact of two revolutions, first the French and then the Industrial. It was a period of violent changes, of vivid contrasts. The rich got richer and the poor got poorer, and a number of creative artists, especially writers, preferred to associate with the latter. Coleridge and Wordsworth, who had been deeply involved in politics, decided in 1800 for a 'humble and rustic life', because 'in that condition the essential passions of the heart find a better soil in which they can attain their maturity, are under less restraint, and speak a

The Banqueting Room, from Nash's 'Views of the Royal Pavilion', Brighton, 1824

plainer and more emphatic language.' The language had to be plainer because the audience was larger.

If one philosophy gained more support than another in the early nineteenth century, it was that of Jeremy Bentham who put forward the principle of Utility: 'the greatest happiness of the greatest number is the foundation of morals and legislation.' On the face of it, this appears a reasonable attitude, and it did much to encourage social reform, but sometimes Bentham reduced it to absurdity. It followed, he said, that 'the game of push-pin is of equal value with the arts and sciences of music and poetry. If the game of push-pin furnishes more pleasure, it is more valuable than either.'

Never did the Philistines have a more eloquent spokesman. As a poet, Coleridge could hardly agree with him there, but he did conclude that if every man maintained a policy of enlightened self-interest, the result would be general happiness. Such a plan would have suited the government (or most of it) very well. 'Laissez-faire' was a comfortable doctrine. 'Men can scarcely create abundance where Providence has inflicted scarcity', said Henry Addington in 1812; so there was no need for him to try. But if the government was apathetic, everyone else was in a fury of endeavour. Robert Owen, for instance, was aiming to found a New Jerusalem—not like Blake with bow of burning gold and arrows of desire, but through a system of co-operative industry at an expense of £80 a head. 'A species of Monkery,' Cobbett called it.

There was in the early nineteenth century a lively and vociferous minority of non-Christians, superior not in numbers but in influence. In France, being a philosopher was almost the same thing as being an atheist. In Britain, the manufacturers and even the landed gentry were beginning to turn away from the church (even if they still expected their wives and children to attend). The new industrial communities were neglected by the established church in Protestant countries, and yet at the same time, it was a great age for foreign missions, and for the establishment of new sects, especially in America.

It was a period then when there were no generally accepted tenets of belief. The old order was upset and men were searching for something to put in its place. Thinking men tended increasingly to look to nature as a guide and source of inspiration, whether it was regarded as a 'collective idea' (as it was by the painter Fuseli), or as a struggle of the elements (as it was by Turner), or as a visionary revelation (as it was by Wordsworth).

One cannot say that many of these ideas were expressed directly in the applied arts. After all, if intellectual and creative men took to simple living and high thinking, they were not much concerned with the design of their chairs and their tea-cups. The workers in the applied arts therefore continued to look for patronage towards those who still had the money and the power to indulge themselves. And since the taste of these men was as diverse and contradictory as the opinions of the philosophers, this was a period of rapidly succeeding—indeed of overlapping—phases.

First, there was neo-classicism, a survival from the previous century. But the style had nearly worn itself out. The style we call 'Empire', current on the continent at the time of Napoleon, was faithful to the letter rather than to the spirit of ancient classical art. It became pompous, heavy, extravagant, full of symbols (imperial eagles, laurel wreaths and such), and derivative—chairs, for instance, were based on what were hoped to be classical models. And art was too frequently used as a form of propaganda for republicanism, or Napoleonic grandeur.

A few men, such as the architect John Soane, the painter J L David, and the sculptor Canova, had sufficient individuality to use classicism for their own ends, and the movement, though slowly dying, received a late blood-transfusion in the form of the Elgin Marbles. These famous Greek sculptures, brought to Britain from the Parthenon in Athens during the second decade of the century, were not universally welcomed. The poet Byron attacked Lord Elgin bitterly and deplored what he saw as the spoliation of the most celebrated of Greek temples. Others, like the writer Hazlitt, hoped that the marbles might lift the arts 'out of the limbo of

Above The Royal Academy, London, from Pugin and
Rowlandson's 'Microcosm of London', 1808. The interior is
that of Somerset House, where exhibitions were then held

Below Design for a monument to Princess Charlotte, by
Charles R Cockerell, pen and wash drawing, 1818

vanity and affectation ... in which they have lain sprawling and fluttering, gasping for breath, wasting away, vapid and abortive.' Elgin himself thought that they might serve as useful models for the applied arts: 'The very great variety in our manufactures, in objects either of elegance or luxury, offers a thousand applications for such details. A chair, a footstool, designs or shapes for porcelain, ornaments for cornices, nothing is indifferent.' If the sculptures did not on the whole have the desired revivifying effect, the fault lay in the calibre of the artists concerned.

Variations from the purely classical were made. There was the Egyptian cult, which flourished after Napoleon's campaigns on the Nile. 'Think of it, soldiers,' said Napoleon before the Battle of the Pyramids, in 1789, 'from the summit of these pyramids, forty centuries look down on you.' Whether the soldiers thought of it or not is unrecorded, but the designers were impressed and the sphinx and the lotus became fashionable devices.

A taste for the exotic also flaunted itself in the 'Chinese' and 'Indian' styles. The 'Indian' was an innovation, and never did it find such extreme and extraordinary form as in the Royal Pavilion at Brighton, designed for the Prince Regent (later George IV) by John Nash. The chinoiserie within, with its bamboo furniture, vivid wallpaper, colourful banners and lanterns, has a new barbaric splendour, far removed from the delicate decorations of eighteenth-century style.

Designers in the early part of the nineteenth century had to be very versatile. Patrons would often request drawings of treatments in different styles—Classical, Chinese, Gothic—all for the same commission. But it was the Gothic style which finally won the day.

The cult of the Gothic penetrated almost all the arts. Mainly it took the form of a revival of German medievalism—or rather, of an enhanced idea of it. There was something fascinating about those dark, mysterious forests and impossibly pinnacled castles. The Middle Ages, as long as they were interestingly and not crudely primitive, were in favour. A long and varied list of works bears this out: the Grimm brothers' *Fairy Tales*, the ballet 'Giselle', Château-briand's *Génie du Christianisme*, the mock-medieval 'Ossian' poems and the poems of Keats and Chatterton, Victor Hugo's *Hunchback of Notre Dame*, and all the buildings and designs of Pugin. Pugin was a Roman Catholic and thoroughly imbued with Gothic idealism, but an influential body of the Church of England also approved of this revival, and only the nonconformist sects clung with any firmness to the classical style.

The Gothic style in design was closely paralleled by Romanticism in literature and indeed in painting. Both required a similar way of looking at things. But the revival of Gothic involved imitation, deliberate archaism; and if it was not used with skill and perhaps also with a sense of humour, its sublimity—to reiterate Napoleon—was only a step from the ridiculous.

Opposite page right French secrétaire, mahogany with white Carrara marble top. Paris, 1804. Ordered by Napoleon for St. Cloud

Opposite page left Austrian mahogany table with gilt bronze mounts, top of semi-precious stone, Vienna, 1800

Furniture

Because of the expense of the Napoleonic wars, furniture during this period tends to reflect, both on the continent and in Britain, the necessity of economy. Even when the general effect is one of richness, the means used are relatively inexpensive: veneers rather than solid timber when a particular wood was costly, and metal decoration rather than carving.

In France, during the period of the Consulate (1799–1804), when the power and prestige of Napoleon were steadily increasing, furniture was light but severe in line. Ornamentation was restrained, and usually reflected the current interest in archaeology, principally Greek. Sometimes classical precedents also affected the forms of furniture: chairs would be made with their back legs sabre-shaped in the Greek manner, though these were commonly combined with spindle-shaped front legs in an uneasy juxtaposition. The backs of chairs were rectangular and generally curved backwards, terminating in a scroll.

Beds at this time were often tent-like, a curious blending of a medieval-type pavilion with decoration in the classical manner. It is possible that the fashion was made popular by Napoleon's camping out while on campaigns. If the hero of France could manage with a tent, then surely the citizens at home could, too–so

from initial hardship evolved high fashion. Small occasional tables were made, often three-legged, and rectangular-topped desks with drop-fronts.

The Consulate merges almost imperceptibly into the Empire style. Gradually furniture became more lavish, more extravagant in form. Cabinet-makers prospered under the new imperial patronage. Designs became increasingly symbolic and theatrical, reflecting Napoleon's aspirations to the grandeur of ancient Rome. Nearly all the furniture designers were architects: for instance, Percier and Fontaine, whose pattern-book full of classical motifs was first published in 1801, and re-issued in 1812. The designs were executed by fashionable cabinet-makers such as Jacob-Desmalter; he designed Empress Josephine's bed.

The woods used during this period were sometimes mahogany–although no mahogany could be imported into France from British possessions after 1806–and sometimes native woods such as beech, which would take gilding successfully. By the end of the Empire period, furniture varied between the uncompromisingly four-square and the opulently exotic.

The wars over and the monarchy restored, the style of furniture changed yet again. Light-coloured native woods were in favour, especially bird's-eye maple. A certain degree of mechanisation crept in, and furniture was made

more for ordinary people than for court taste. Finally there came a fashion for Gothic. Chairs were pinnacled like miniature cathedrals, and dark woods came back into favour.

As one might expect, the French Empire style was closely followed by almost all those countries which came-under Napoleon's domination: Germany, Austria and Italy, for instance. In the two former areas, it was followed by a simpler and essentially middle-class style, the 'Biedermeyer'. Functional and reticent, Biedermeyer owes much to English taste. But by about 1840, the Gothic became fashionable there too.

Meanwhile, England retained her independence in furniture design as in politics. At the beginning of the century, there was an increasing interest in all things Greek, and details from the Parthenon cornices appeared as embellishments to furniture and interior decoration. The scene was dominated by the architect Henry Holland, who was responsible for the redecoration of Carlton House for the Prince Regent (later George IV) and of Woburn for the Duke of Bedford. There was a preference for dark woods–rosewood from Brazil, kingwood also

from South America, as well as the ever-popular mahogany. Largely they were used in the form of veneers, and contrasted with ormolu mounts (as in France) and brass inlays.

The next influential figure was that of Thomas Hope, who published his *Household Furniture* in 1807. Hope had spent eight years studying the archaeology and architecture of the Eastern Mediterranean. He advocated a thoughtful and scholarly revival of ancient styles. In *Household Furniture* he recommended 'that breadth and repose of surface . . . that harmony and significance of accessories, and that apt accord between the peculiar meaning of each imitative and significant detail and the peculiar destination of the main object . . . which are calculated to afford to the eye and mind the most lively, most permanent and most unfading enjoyment.' Hope executed his furniture in accordance with these principles, and the result is rather ponderous. He had a follower in George Smith, who seems to have worked with Hope's ideas in mind, and on occasion copied his designs.

Nelson's victory at the Nile in 1798, and also the publication of Denon's *Travels in Lower and*

English gilt chair in 'Gothic taste', upholstered in brown velvet with silk embroidery, about 1825–30

English carved oak chair by Pugin, about 1840

Inlaid circular table from Thomas Hope's 'Household Furniture', 1807

Upper Egypt in 1802, stimulated a taste for Egyptian art. Hope warned against the ignorant use of its forms, such as hieroglyphics; but the Egyptian style flourished (cabinet-makers paying little regard to symbolism) until about 1830.

The vogue for Chinese and *chinoiserie* stemmed mainly from the taste of King George IV. In 1802, when he was still Prince of Wales, he had been sent some exquisite Chinese wallpaper for Brighton Pavilion, which was just being re-modelled. He was so impressed that he decided to have his new decorations and furniture designed to go with the wallpaper. The furniture was mostly made between 1815 and 1822 by the firm of Crace and Robert Jones. Sometimes genuine oriental lacquer panels were incorporated.

Finally there came the vogue for Gothic. As early as 1808, George Smith had been singing its praises, for it was capable, he said, of 'a more abundant variety of ornaments and forms than

can possibly be attained in any other style.' Gothic was especially popular for book-cases and library furniture, generally in oak. In 1829, Augustus Charles Pugin (father of the architect A W Pugin) published his book *Gothic Furniture*, and the style was really under weigh.

There were technical as well as stylistic changes during this period. 'French polish', which brought out the grain of the wood and gave it a glossy surface far less laboriously than had been possible up to this time, was introduced shortly after the Napoleonic Wars. There were also the first attempts at mechanization. For instance, wood-cutting machinery was installed in the house of the philosopher Jeremy Bentham by his brother Samuel—enough, one would have thought, to tax any philosopher's philosophical calm. But from these small beginnings the industry of furniture-making was to evolve, and the craft of it, on the whole, to decline.

Ceramics

Not even the most avid enthusiast for nineteenth-century art could deny that as far as ceramics were concerned, the first forty years were a period of decline. It was not only that the old type of patronage was disappearing fast and countless factories (in particular those producing porcelain) closed down towards the end of the eighteenth century. More fundamentally it was that the structure of society had changed, ways of thinking had also changed, and the spirit of the age no longer found its supreme expression in porcelain.

In France, the workers of the Sèvres porcelain factory had endured a difficult and penurious time during the Revolution. During the Napoleonic era they did better; the factory was re-organised under Alexandre Brongniart and enjoyed imperial patronage. Large orders were received from Napoleon for wares recording and commemorating military events. The form and decorative qualities of the vessels and plates were considered hardly as important as the scenes and symbols depicted on them. These magnificent services of porcelain, such as that recalling the Egyptian Campaign (Napoleon took it with him to St Helena; it is now in the possession of the Louvre in Paris), were certainly very skilfully painted. Scenes of, for instance, pyramids and palms were set in reserve panels; much gilding was used to embellish the rest of the piece.

By this time the Sèvres factory had adopted the hard-paste formula, and soft-paste was no longer made. The hard-paste had great strength and brilliance. Sometimes undecorated pieces were made which were, unfortunately, decorated elsewhere in over-glaze colours. Some of the early-nineteenth-century Sèvres pieces are charming and lively in decoration, but they have not quite the springing and delicate forms of the earlier wares.

In Italy, the Capodimonte factory in Naples continued under royal patronage until 1806. The porcelain included some attractive figure-groups of ordinary townspeople, made in soft porcelain. The factory was then taken into private hands until it closed in 1834, but produced little of merit. In Russian porcelain centres, at St Petersburg and just outside Moscow, French Empire styles prevailed. In Russia, whatever was French was fashionable. In Denmark, the Copenhagen factory also followed the Empire style, until with the advent of the sculptor Thorvaldsen in 1835 new Greek Revival models were introduced.

British porcelain had always been a matter of private enterprise, so there were no dramatic changes in the type of patronage. The main innovation in the early nineteenth century was the development of 'bone china' (the name derives from the bone-ash employed) which became, and still is, the standard British porcelain body. Bone-ash had been used before in England and was a constituent of the porcelain body made at Bow from the mid-eighteenth century – contemporaries commenting on its strength and cheapness. Nineteenth-century 'bone china' is a development from the Bow formula. The credit for it usually goes to Josiah Spode in Staffordshire. Certainly, at this time, Staffordshire became the main centre for all types of ceramics. Innumerable small porcelain factories now sprang up, and the only major factories outside Staffordshire which continued to produce porcelain were at Derby and Worcester.

At Worcester, a particularly fine white porcelain was developed by William Billingsley. He had had his own pottery at Pinxton near Nottingham. He left Worcester for Wales and again founded his own factory at Nantgarw, and then transferred to Swansea. Apart from the excellent quality of the body of his china, Billingsley is chiefly remembered for his individual handling of painted flower decoration. The Swansea factory closed in 1826. At Coalport, there developed around 1830 an attempt at a revival of rococo decoration. Elaborate vases were made with coloured flowers in high relief—somewhat over-opulent for modern taste, but a considerable technical achievement.

In the field of earthenware, transfer-printing was developed. It was associated especially with Liverpool. Since the principle purpose of the technique was cheapness, transfer-printing kept in the main to a single-colour process. Blue was the favourite colour, printed on to a white ground, but other colours were also used.

The Wedgwood factory (nothing if not conservative) were still producing their famous 'jasper' stoneware. By about 1840, ceramics were beginning to reflect the new vogue for the Gothic revival, as is illustrated in the white stoneware jugs by Charles Meigh of Hanley.

English 'Minster' jug in 'Gothic taste', by Charles Meigh of Hanley, White stoneware, about 1840

Opposite page Welsh soft porcelain dish, decorated in enamel colours and gilt, by William Billingsley at Swansea, about 1820

107

Silver

The dominating figure of the period in England is that of Paul Storr, considered to be the last of the great British goldsmiths. Much of the royal silver is by his hand, because King George IV (who took more than a passing interest in aesthetic matters) decided to commission him to re-model it. This we should call regrettable, however much we may admire the work of Storr, but the value of silver was then held to lie only in the intrinsic worth of the metal – they had no qualms about melting down pieces of

bygone design, the important thing was to be in the current fashion. Storr's work tends towards the massive and grandiloquent. Sometimes he used the designs of celebrated artists such as the classical sculptor John Flaxman.

In France, Napoleon naturally needed impressive silver to fulfil his notions of grandeur. Such a piece is the 'cadena' made for the Empress Josephine. (It was the custom that at a state banquet royalty should have their own place-setting, or cadena, in front of them. This took the form of a raised tray, elaborately ornamented, with boxes for condiments, so that the regal

Above The Malmaison Cadena: plate-stand made for the Empress Josephine, 1804. The compartments are for salt, pepper or spice

Opposite page top French silver salt-cellar, partly gilt. One of a set of six made by J-B-C Odiot, possibly for a gift from Napoleon to the Dutch ambassador in France, 1798–1809

Opposite page below English silver sugar bowl, 1803, chased with the arms of the City of London, by Digby Scott and Benjamin Smith

personage would not have to ask anyone to pass the salt, but would have an individual supply.) On both sides of the Channel, much heavily symbolic work was made – in France it might be a massive urn with imperial emblems, in England a tremendous candelabra to commemorate the victories of Nelson or Wellington.

The most fashionable silversmith in Paris was probably Martin-Guillaume Biennais, who produced pieces of suave and rounded form and liked to work on a lavish scale. Some of the

In France, Napoleon naturally needed impressive silver to fulfil his notions of grandeur.

English silver-gilt fruit-basket on stand, by Paul Storr, 1810

Glass

In general, the early nineteenth century was a period of technical advance for glass. Vessels became thicker, heavier, and were often decorated by cutting.

In Bohemia and Germany, glass was made to resemble semi-precious stones, in particular agate. This was the invention of Friedrich Egermann, who was also responsible for the development of coloured glass, yellow-stained from about 1820 onwards, and red from 1840. Engraved glass was also popular; an engraver by the name of Dominik Birmann did a roaring trade at the spa of Franzensbad, engraving portrait heads of the visitors. Anton Kothgasser specialised in decorating glasses with miniature painting, while the Mohn family, notably Gottlob Samuel Mohn (who had begun as a porcelain painter) did transparent painting on glass.

In France, engraving was the most popular decorative technique. Some engravers from Bohemia were to be found working in Paris, but the most important Frenchman in this field was Charpentier, whose Empire-style glasses engraved with goddesses and *putti* date from between 1813 and 1819.

Ireland specialised in cut glass. The factory which had been founded by English glass-makers at Waterford continued under another Englishman, a Quaker by the name of Jonathan Gatchell. He was first employed there as a clerk, but had control of the business from 1810 until his death in 1825. Excellent quality flint glass was

Above Bohemian painted beaker by Gottlob Samuel Mohn of Vienna, about 1800

Above right Glass seal, American, representing cornerstone laid by Lafayette, dated June 17 1825

Below Silver tea service by Samuel Kirk of Baltimore, 1828

also made at Cork, especially at the Waterloo Glass Company works between 1815 and 1835. A variety of wares were made at both centres, also some at Dublin. There were decanters, wineglasses and all manner of tableware, lustres and lamps, and cutting was the favourite decorative technique.

This was also so in England. Chandeliers during the Regency period became increasingly large and elaborate. Formerly chandeliers had been designed with a slim central shaft and curving branches sprouting from it. Now both shaft and branches became submerged under swags of pendant lustres, and the shape of the chandelier was conceived as a whole.

America was responsible for the invention of pressed glass. The glass industry in America was growing rapidly. In 1800 there were only nine glasshouses, but by 1837 there were 100. The first known patent for pressed glass was issued on 9 September 1825 to John P Bakewell of Pittsburgh, for the manufacture of furniture knobs. The earliest hollow pressed glass was made by Enoch Robinson of Cambridge, Massachusetts, and Deming Jarves of Boston. It became a speciality of the Boston & Sandwich Glass Company at Sandwich, Massachusetts, and is commonly known as Sandwich glass. Some of the pressed pieces were made to resemble cut glass (pressing was a much cheaper technique), some had the beaded and relief decoration known as the 'Lacy' pattern. Glass lamps were made as well as tableware, but earlier than the 1820s these were free-blown. Around 1830, it was common for the bowl of the lamp to be made of blown and the base of pressed glass.

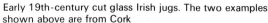

Early 19th-century cut glass Irish jugs. The two examples shown above are from Cork

English glass chandelier from Wroxton Abbey, about 1815

English Regency Interiors
Opposite page, above The King's Bedroom, the Royal
Pavilion, Brighton, completed in 1821. The bed is carved
mahogany

Opposite page, below The Music Room, from Nash's
'Views of the Royal Pavilion', Brighton, 1824

Above The Blue Velvet Room, Carlton House, 1816. A
watercolour by C Wild

Bracket clock, ebony veneer on oak; movement by John Knibb, Oxford, about 1700

Left Long case clock, oak lacquered with Chinese Gothic and Georgian motifs, designed by John Ellicott (1706–1772). Mid-18th century

Top 19th century Act of Parliament clock. The case is papier mâché

Above Ebonised wood clock, incised decoration, sunflower dial, about 1880

117

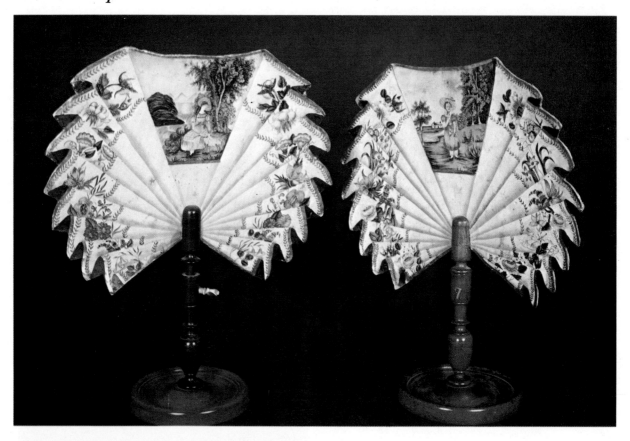

Above Pair of American painted candle-shades

Left Staffordshire figure group of Napoleon III and the Empress Eugénie, about 1860

Opposite page English porcelain: Coalport vase with applied floral decoration, about 1830

1840–1910

'To understand a work of art, an artist, a group of artists,' wrote the French philosopher and critic Hippolyte Taine, 'one needs an exact picture of the general state of mind and way of life to which they belong.' Taine took this idea (which was a new one) further, and argued that a work of art is in fact the product of its environment. Today we might think that this was overstating the case, but we would agree that we get more pleasure from a work of art if we know something about how people thought and lived when it was made.

And what was the state of mind and way of life in the middle years of the nineteenth century? In material terms, most people were better off than they had been before. Food was cheaper, the average wage was higher and the mortality rate lower. Education–in some countries–was beginning to be the concern of the state. There was less crime, less drunkenness. Especially in Britain, respectability and cleanliness were the favourite virtues. The railway system was developing fast. There was a greater range of goods to buy in the shops, and industrialized production ensured that they were not over-expensive. It was, as Thomas Carlyle described it, 'An Age of Machinery, in every outward and inward sense of that word.'

However, it was not a golden age. Machinery could in itself lead to unemployment, and pathetic little documents survive to testify to the exploitation of the very poor. An age in which boys were employed to open the doors of iron furnaces, or lost their jaws from dipping matches into phosphorus, in which girls worked twelve hours a day in steamy lace-houses or muddy brickfields, and women made shirts at home for as little as 4s6d a dozen, was not what we should call golden. Genteelly brought up people were hardly expected to know these facts, still less to do anything about them. The Industrial Revolution, then in full swing in Britain and Germany and gathering momentum in America, had certainly brought about an increase in material prosperity. Production was the key-word, time must not be wasted. 'Be no longer

The Drawing Room, Penrhyn Castle, Caernarvonshire, Wales

a chaos, but a world,' wrote Thomas Carlyle, 'Produce! Produce! Were it but the pitifullest infinitesimal fraction of a product, produce it in God's name! 'Tis the utmost thou hast in thee: out with it, then.'

For all this activity and prosperity, it was not a happy age. 'I know not why I am so sad,' wrote the German poet Heinrich Heine, 'I cannot get out of my head a fairy-tale of olden times.' After the widespread revolutions of 1848 had fizzled out like a packet of damp squibs, pessimism set in. There was a feeling of failure and disillusionment. It was only science that inspired confidence.

As for industry, it was a luxuriant growth which, it was felt, might be trained by art into a more elegant shape. Mass production methods, it was feared, were encouraging copying, and the manufacturers might be copying the wrong things. The solution was thought to be to found in museums of art where the good designs of the past might be collected, preserved and studied. When the founding of the National Gallery, London, was first discussed in Parliament, Sir Robert Peel said: **It is well known that our manufacturers were, in all matters connected with machinery, superior to all their foreign competitors; but in the pictorial designs, which were so important in recommending the productions of industry to the taste of the consumer, they were, unfortunately, not equally successful; and hence they have found themselves unequal to cope with their rivals. This deserved the serious consideration of the House in its patronage of the fine arts.**

The National Gallery, and later the Victoria and Albert Museum, came into being. One might say that the right deed had been done for the wrong reason. There was too much emphasis on copying. A man might go to South Kensington, find a design which seemed to him exciting or exotic or even, in plain terms, useful, and apply it to a shape or a medium for which it had never been intended. It was nothing new for a design to be derivative; the fault was that it was now thoughtlessly derivative. Work of this kind abounded in the Great Exhibition held in Hyde Park, London, in 1851. Financially this was a great success; some of the

121

Top left Chair by H Eyles of Bath, the plaque of Queen Victoria in Worcester porcelain, 1851

Opposite page, top 'Mr. and Mrs. Carlyle at Home' by Robert Tait, 1858

Top right Embroidered screen, probably by William Morris, about 1860

Opposite page, below English Gothic-style sideboard, by Philip Webb, about 1862

Left and above William Morris designs for wallpaper, 'Blackthorn', 1892 and chintz, 'Strawberry Thief'

profits bought land on which the South Kensington Museums, including the Victoria and Albert, stand; some founded the Rome scholarships in the Fine Arts. The Exhibition was remarkable in being an international one, and its organization was carried out, not without opposition, but with a splendid confidence. Henry Cole, its principal promoter, declared: **The history of the world records no event comparable in its promotion of human industry, with that of the Great Exhibition of the Works of Industry of all Nations in 1851. A great people invited all civilized nations to a festival, to bring into comparison the works of human skill. It was carried out by its own private means; was self-supporting and independent of taxes and the employment of slaves, which great works had exacted in ancient days. A prince of pre-eminent wisdom, of philosophic mind, sagacity, with power of generalship and great practical ability, placed himself at the head of the enterprise, and led it to triumphant success.**

We may find much to criticise and to ridicule in the Great Exhibition, and feel that the 'Crystal Palace', which Joseph Paxton designed to house it, far outshone any of the exhibits, but this brain-child of the Prince Consort's was a truly amazing creature.

The Tower Room, Cardiff Castle, by William Burges,
1870–75: an attempt to re-create medievalism

The Hall, Adcote, Shropshire, by Norman Shaw,
1879: an evocation of the Gothic Spirit

Queen Victoria, who was a constant visitor to the Exhibition, pronounced it most gratifying to see the 'immense improvement in taste in all the manufactures.' William Morris was only a boy at the time, but would scarcely have agreed with her. Writing towards the end of the century, he abhorred both the industrial system of the time and the works it produced. He conjured up a vision of an ideal factory in a garden setting, where healthy craftsmen rejoiced in their work. Morris was fascinated by the dream of a medieval never-never-land. He was, however, a great champion of the applied arts (he desired to equate them with the fine arts; indeed, he felt the distinction was a false one), and looked for their revival. This would depend firstly on the study of nature, he said, and secondly on the study of works in galleries and museums. 'If you can really fill your minds with memories of great works of art, and great times of art, you will . . . be moved to discontent of what is careless and brutal now, and will, I hope, at last be so much discontented with what is bad, that you will determine to bear no longer that shortsighted, reckless brutality of squalor that so disgraces our intricate civilization.' Art of the people, by the people and for the people was his dream; aesthetic doctrines in Morris were mixed up with political beliefs, and he was a romantic Radical.

Above Copper box with brass and enamel: Art Nouveau design of Celtic inspiration

Left English Art Nouveau clock in pewter and enamel case: a 'Tudric' design from Liberty's

Opposite page, top Project by Charles Rennie Mackintosh for the Music Room of an 'Art-lover's house', 1901

Opposite page, below Art Nouveau at its most elongated and approaching 20th-century design with its geometrical lines

There is no doubt that Morris was a potent and on the whole a beneficial influence on the applied arts. Some of his wallpaper designs, for instance, have never been surpassed. He was very closely associated with the Pre-Raphaelite artists (Rossetti for instance) whom he sometimes persuaded to turn from easel-painting to decorating his handicrafts. Rossetti was a passionate if indiscriminating collector of antiques and kept them in a wild profusion. The American painter Whistler, on the other hand, introduced a taste for the oriental which involved not only the acquisition of Japanese fans, screens and prints and Chinese 'blue-and-white' porcelain, but–in Whistler's case–a calculated and courageous use of space in design.

A tiny minority followed this principle of art for art's sake, whereby all judgements became aesthetic ones. Walter Pater was one of them. The heir to all this aestheticism was the young and shortlived artist Aubrey Beardsley (1872–1898). His exquisite though decadent drawings, especially those in the first issue of 'The Studio', may, together with the works of William Morris and his circle, be said to be the fore-runners of the style known as Art Nouveau.

Art Nouveau was a curious style, or rather mixture of styles, whose influence is with us still. The general public did not readily take to Art Nouveau, partly because the artists were seldom willing to compromise to suit the requirements of industrial production, partly because the designs were often too alien to be acceptable. This saddened William Morris and he broke with the movement. Moreover, he saw in Beardsley's 'Morte d'Arthur' drawings

The Mackintosh Room, Glasgow School of Art.
This was formerly the Board Room, designed by
Mackintosh in 1897–9

a cruel parody of his own love for a medieval ideal. Morris became the revered father of the Arts and Crafts movement, which existed alongside Art Nouveau. Again it was a minority affair, but better liked in Britain because it seemed more cranky than sinful. The aim was, as Walter Crane expressed it, 'to turn our artists into craftsmen and our craftsmen into artists.'

Even though it was not, to begin with, an expression of public taste, Art Nouveau spread rapidly across Europe and to America, and affected all the visual arts. But was it a 'new art', as the name suggests? In fact it drew very much from rococo design, from Celtic, Tudor, and Japanese. Nevertheless the artists felt themselves to be departing from tradition. They were rebelling against obvious naturalism, and seeking organic forms, a visual expression of creation and growth.

This was true of all Art Nouveau designs, as long as they were not secondhand and debased; yet, starting from this common root, they developed in different ways. Sometimes they had the complex linear rhythms of, say, a fabric design by Mackmurdo, or an interior by Horta. Sometimes they took on the vertical forms characteristic of the work of Charles Rennie Mackintosh, sometimes the weightiness favoured by the Vienna Secession movement in Austria. But this the artists had in common: that they were trying to express something which was felt rather than something which was observed.

French Art Nouveau interior: the Magasin Vaxelaire, Nancy, by Emile André & Vallin, 1902. The furnishings are clearly designed to go with the room

Furniture

'Glaring, showy and meretricious ornament was never so much in vogue as at present' declared A W Pugin whose *True Principles of Christian Architecture* came out in 1841. He was trying to replace the 'sprawling Rococo' of his age with a more rational type of furniture based on simplified Gothic lines. The sprawling Rococo, however, continued, along with a revival of Tudor, classical and 'Gothick' styles; the numerous pattern-books provided the designers with a very handy guide. In France, there was much copying of furniture from all the great periods of French furniture. In England, the straighter lines of the eighteenth century were not in favour until after about 1865. In both countries there was a liking for opulent and curvaceous upholstery, in both a general desire to impress. This was evident in and encouraged by the Great Exhibition in 1851. Pieces of enormous size were made and large mirrors were much in vogue. There were new techniques too, such as papier-mâché; the compressed paper was generally enamelled and often inlaid with mother-of-pearl. Papier-mâché was generally used only for small pieces such as chairs, but for the Exhibition some large virtuoso furniture incorporated this material. In America, a new mid-century style was the so-called Elizabethan—which in fact, with its characteristic turned legs, owed far more to the seventeenth century. This existed alongside the seemingly ever-popular rococo. In Britain there was,

American half-tester bed, designed by Prudent Mallard in the Louis XV style, mid-19th century

English bedstead, Japanned
metal with papier mâché
panels about 1850

however, a tendency to straighten out the lines
of furniture during the second half of the century,
and the 1870s saw the rise of the Free Renaissance (or 'bracket-and-overmantel') style—still
heavy in line, although sometimes remarkable
for its craftsmanship.

Reformers like A W Pugin, and later, William
Morris, whose firm was founded in 1861, were
aiming to produce a rational and less expensive
type of furniture, something which ordinary
people could buy. In part they were successful,
but Morris's dream of a factory as it might be
never materialised and the best furniture continued to be made by hand and therefore tended
to be expensive. As well as highly wrought
pieces, inlaid and perhaps painted by the Pre-
Raphaelite artists with literary and medieval

scenes. Morris's firm did, however, design some
simpler ones such as the Sussex chair, a variation
on country Windsor. In 1888, Ernest Gimson
followed this up with his new style ladder-
back. There was a revival of craftsmanship.
Good craftsmanship was the basic tenet of the
Century Guild founded in 1882 (with Mackmurdo, Voysey and Ashbee), and indeed of the
whole Arts and Crafts movement. It was a
reaction against industrialism, rather than an
attempt to reform it.

Although the influence of Japanese art from
the 1870s onwards led to some lightening of
colour and design, most nineteenth-century
interiors were dark and heavy. Morris's certainly
were. The cry 'Let some light in!' came from
Carl Larsson of Sweden (1899). At the same time,

English copy of a Boulle writing-table with clock, veneered
on oak with ebony, coromandel-wood and Boulle marquetry,
bronze mounts. The original was made about 1715 for the
Elector of Bavaria; this copy, 1855-7, for the Marquess of
Hertford

English revival of late medieval styles: cabinet designed
in the 15th-century manner by Pugin, about 1852

English cabinet, oak inlaid with other woods and painted
by Madox Brown, Burne-Jones, Rossetti and Morris with
scenes from Scott's 'Anna von Geierstein'

English cradle decorated with the signs of the zodiac, by
Norman Shaw, 1861

the Art Nouveau designers were dispelling some of the encircling gloom. The Norwegian Gerhard Munthe was producing furniture of a peasant-like gaiety. Charpentier in France was designing pieces which even if they seem to us perversely convoluted at least were not heavy or pedestrian. Riemerschmid shook free from antiquarianism and produced furniture astonishingly modern in form. Charles Rennie Mackintosh's elongated shapes, while they appealed to a discerning few in Glasgow, were little regarded in Britain as a whole, but they had immediate impact on design in Austria. The Vienna Secession designers such as Josef Hoffmann emulated his cleanness of line although they did not achieve his elegance. Art Nouveau expressed itself in furniture as a truly international style, but one to which artists from different countries brought distinctly national contributions.

Chair with ladder back, designed by Ernest Gimson, 1888

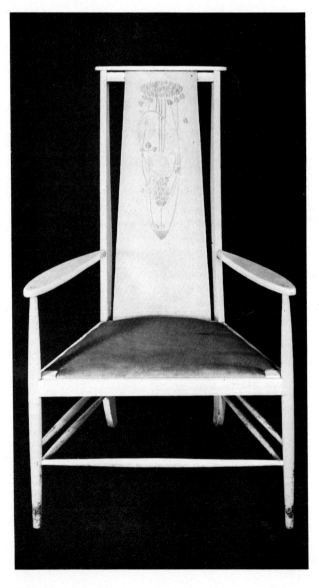

Left White painted chair designed by Charles Rennie Mackintosh for the Willow Tea-rooms, Glasgow, about 1900

Ceramics

This was a period when technically potters were capable of almost anything–and so they were, unfortunately, in matters of design. It was generally held that the more elaborate a piece was, the more difficult and costly it was to produce, the more desirable it must be. Luckily, not quite all manufacturers of pottery believed this. For one reason or another, plainer wares were made which, to our eyes, seem more pleasing than the excessive effusions thought then to be masterpieces.

It was the height of good taste, most people thought, in decorating ceramics to revive some historical style. In the 1840s, Gothic was all the vogue; the fashion even spread to America, and stoneware jugs with Gothic relief panels were made, very much on the English pattern.

With the founding of museums, the copying of past styles became temptingly easy. Wedgwood jasper-ware continued to indulge a taste for classical antiquarianism (although occasionally realistic plant-forms were favoured instead). Now the fashion spread, and other potteries took it up, mostly in Staffordshire but also at Swansea, where so-called Etruscan wares were made, based on Greek 'red-figure' painted vases. The second half of the century saw a revival of Renaissance styles. The best pieces were done in Italy, where potteries such as Cantigalli produced cunning reproductions of fifteenth and sixteenth century maiolica, but creditable attempts were also made by Minton in England.

Minton pottery was nothing if not versatile. 'Parian' ware was made, a white porcelain imitating marble, mainly used for statuettes. Then in 1871, an 'Art-Pottery Studio' was set up in Kensington, and artists, many of them easel-painters, were given plain wares to decorate–the idea was that the fine arts might serve to improve the useful.

In France, meanwhile, there was a fashion to revive the reptile-infested high reliefs of Bernard Palissy, and the porcelain manufacturers of Sèvres were busy elaborating a nineteenth-century version of rococo–curvaceous, but lacking the grace of the real thing.

Top Welsh earthenware vase by Dillwyn of Swansea, inspired by ancient Greek pottery, about 1850

Right American pitcher with Gothic relief panels, Rockingham type glaze, made by the American Pottery Co., Jersey City, between 1838 and 1845

The Japanese vogue of the 1870s produced some very accomplished pieces. They were in our judgement most successful when the potter concentrated on emulating the subtleties of form and glaze, rather than copying surface painting of which he seldom understood the significance. The Japanese-style pieces paved the way for Art Nouveau. As far as ceramics was concerned, the Art Nouveau style affected decoration rather than form. The design might be stressed by the use of relief lines, but the basic shape of the pot remained unchanged.

As a reaction against the over-mechanization of pottery, there began a line of artist-potters, a tradition which is continued to this day. Unlike the 'Art-Pottery Studio' painters of Minton wares, these men were directly concerned with every process in the making of a pot, from the first flinging of wet clay on to the wheel. An early pioneer in France was Théodore Deck, and Ernest Chaplet excelled in developing glazing techniques. In England, there was an interesting collaboration between the Doulton factory and the Lambeth School of Art, and among the William Morris circle there was William de Morgan. More of a designer than a practising potter, he favoured lustre finishes and an Islamic taste in colouring. Perhaps the most original of these free-lances were the Martin Brothers, who worked vigorously—and sometimes grotesquely—in salt-glazed stoneware; their spiritual descendants are the studio-potters of today.

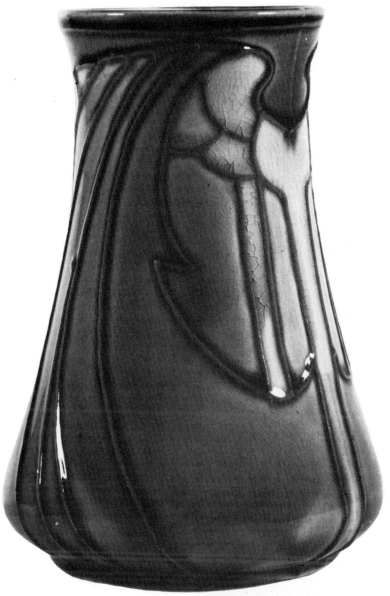

English Art Nouveau vase by Minton, early 20th century

English salt-glazed stoneware vase by the Martin Brothers, Southall, about 1886

Opposite page Italian maiolica dish with grotesque decoration, by Torelli of Florence, about 1875: an attempt to revive Renaissance styles

Silver

Among the exhibits at the 1851 Exhibition was a silver centre-piece made by J Wagner and Son of Prussia, an elaborate fountain-shaped affair with numerous figures around it and an angel at the top. It was annotated thus: 'In it the artist has attempted to portray the progress of man's endeavours to rise, by the subjugation of material nature, to a final triumph over the powers of capital evil.' But this was what man was failing so lamentably to do in the middle years of the nineteenth century. Large symbolic or commemorative pieces were made in silver with little function but to express their owner's prosperity, and it was hoped that if they featured the royal dogs, or the characters of Shakespeare, or the figures of great goldsmiths of the past, this would redeem their lack of distinction in other respects.

As in the other arts, there was a widespread revival of historical styles. Gothic was especially in favour. The silver designed by Pugin shown at the Great Exhibition was said to 'fully realize the style and artistic feeling of the best works of the Middle Ages.' The first step towards reform came, rather surprisingly, from the prime mover of the Exhibition, Sir Henry Cole. Using a pseudonym, he established Felix Summerly's Art Manufactures. Well-known artists were commissioned to design articles for everyday use. The results showed a pleasing blend of form and decoration.

The fluid lines of Art Nouveau expressed themselves very eloquently in silver. The pair of egg-cups in a covered dish, designed by P Wolfers, combine a refreshingly plain interior with an exterior which is almost rococo in its sinuous naturalism. The English designer C R Ashbee, who was primarily an architect, favoured forms of a slender elegance, often closely related to the function of the piece. The Frenchman René Lalique, on the other hand, created richly strange forms sometimes combining silver with glass and his favourite stone, the opal. This was known as his 'tentacular' style.

Opposite page English silver candelabrum, with figures of the goldsmiths Benvenuto Cellini, George Heriot and Sir Martin Bowes round the base. Made in 1853 by Hunt and Roskell

Right Silver bowl, set with semi-precious stone, by C R Ashbee, 1898

Below Silver poacher by Philippe Wolfers (1858–1928): Art Nouveau brought renewed originality to silver design

Mid-19th-century glassware design: a group from the Great Exhibition of 1851 by A Pellatt, W Naylor and J G Green

Glass

'In glass, we cannot equal the ornamental manufactures of Bohemia'; so ran an article in *The Times* for 7 June 1851, commenting on the glassware shown in the Great Exhibition. Much of the admired Bohemian ware was made of cased glass, the outer coloured layer being partly cut away to reveal the opaque white underneath. Also at the Exhibition was colourless cut-glass, very deeply and profusely cut so that the actual shape of the vessel was almost obscured. Cut glass was on the decline, however, possibly due to the rise of pressed glass—which, in public opinion, so nearly approximated to it that the real thing ceased to be valued and only the imitation flourished. Pressed glass was undoubtedly versatile as well as cheap; an enormous variety of forms were made of it, including glass busts which were cast from metal moulds.

As well as these heavier shapes, very light and often elaborately engraved glasses were in vogue, their wide-lipped bowls balanced on improbably fragile stems. Meanwhile there was a revival in France and Germany of glass made in the Venetian manner.

Victorian cut-glass jug in the Bohemian style

In England, shortly after 1851, there developed a cult for cameo-carved glass. Opaque white glass was overlaid on a darker body and then carved into low relief designs resembling cameos. This obviously involved a degree of careful and even tedious craftsmanship. However the cameo-cutters were given added incentive when Benjamin Richardson, a glass-maker from Stourbridge, proposed a reward of £1000 for the nearest reproduction of the famous Portland Vase in this medium. It was won by his former apprentice John Northwood, whose work took him some three years and was completed in 1876. Northwood's achievement rendered the technique fashionable; the subjects

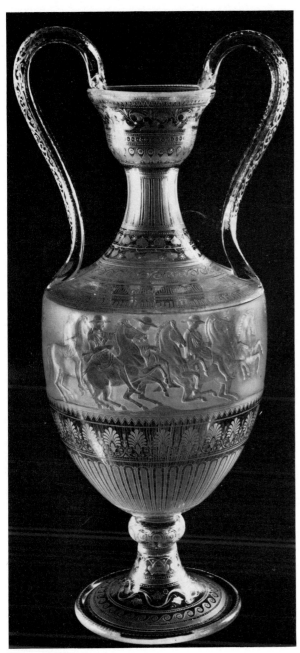

English cameo-carved glass: the Elgin Vase, by John Northwood Senior, 1876

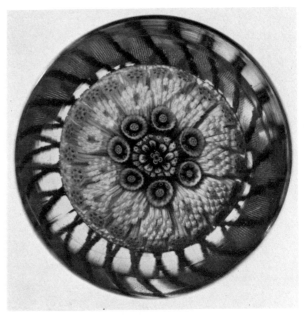

Two Baccarat glass paperweights, mid-19th century. The 'millefiori' (thousand-flower) effect of the piece above was achieved by setting coloured glass rods close together

portrayed were generally from classical mythology, although plant designs were also used.

Such pieces were clearly intended to be admired rather than used. William Morris had protested at the over-elaborate glass displayed at the 1851 Exhibition, and had encouraged glassmakers such as Powell and Northwood to make plainer wares. These were in advance of public taste in the 1860s, but by the last quarter of the century, everyday wine-glasses were being made slender in form and reticent in decoration.

The leaders of the Art Nouveau movement, on the other hand, wanted to use glass as a means of artistic expression, and they were far from reticent about it. Their designs seek to recapture the liquidity of glass in its molten state. They liked to colour it and treat it as something intrinsically precious. Emile Gallé, a Frenchman from Nancy, inspired by the Chinese glass he had seen at the Victoria and Albert Museum on his visit to London in 1871, set up his own factory three years later, producing colour-flashed glasses engraved with plant designs. He also liked to combine glass with metal, or create out of it organic flower formations. 'Our roots,' he said, 'lie at the threshold of the woods, in the moss at the edge of the pond.'

In the United States, the chief exponent in Art Nouveau was Louis Comfort Tiffany. He began as a stained-glass artist, but in 1879 established the Tiffany Studios. There, attempting to re-create the iridescent quality of ancient or decayed glass (he had noted this on his travels in Egypt), he developed in 1893 his 'Favrile' glass. The technique was to reheat the glass after manufacture and spray on salts of iron or tin. This gave it a metallic lustre finish, which was admired and emulated not only in his own country but also among the Vienna Secession designers in Austria.

Great Art Nouveau glassmakers such as Gallé and Tiffany showed a natural feeling for the character of the medium. Inferior copyists of their styles, lacking this feeling, could produce monstrosities. Art Nouveau was, and still is, a very potent influence on the applied arts, and to it may be traced some of the best and worst in modern design: the best shows an understanding of its motives (outlined in the introduction to this chapter), the worst a misapplication of its mannerisms.

Central-European Art Nouveau: globular Bohemian glass bowl, the stem-like mount made in Germany. Designed by P. Wolfers, about 1900

French Art Nouveau vase by Emile Gallé, about 1900

Spanish square piano, by Florez of Madrid, about 1800

Below English Apollo lyres, by Robert Wornum of London, about 1813

Right French pedal harp, by Cousineau of Paris, about 1880

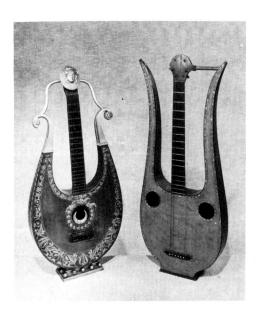